To AJ

THEY CALLED ME THE
HILLSIDE
RAPIST

JAY CHAPMAN

BEAVER'S
POND
PRESS

THEY CALLED ME THE

HILLSIDE

RAPIST

ISBN 13: 978-1-64343-898-6

Library of Congress Catalog Number: 2020914210

Printed in the United States of America
First Printing: 2020
24   23   22   21   20   5   4   3   2   1

Cover and interior design by James Monroe Design, LLC.

Beaver's Pond Press, Inc.
939 Seventh Street West
Saint Paul, Minnesota 55102
(952) 829-8818
www.BeaversPondPress.com

BEAVER'S
POND
PRESS

*The only thing to finally do is to let it out,
let it go, forgive.*

*Only then will you be able to live unashamed
and at peace with yourself.*

Only then will you be free.

—JODY PREIMESBERGER

These feelings are destroying me.

—JAY CHAPMAN

Introduction

This book has been nearly four decades in the making, beginning with a series of brutal sexual assaults and rapes in the Cathedral Hill neighborhood of Saint Paul, Minnesota, in 1981 and 1982.

It was conceived and cowritten by the man who stood accused of the crimes and was researched by the woman who shared his journey until the end of her life in 2016. Both were just kids at the time of the assaults.

In addition to being a recounting of a vicious crime spree, this book is also a love story about those two kids, Jay Chapman and Jody Preimesberger, who met and fell for each other at first sight. Then they stayed together through extraordinary circumstances: a false accusation, imprisonment, and a lifetime of residual shame, blame, and guilt—alongside love, devotion, marriage, children, and divorce.

This book is the distillation of a trunk load of information—literally. Over the years letters written from jail, diary and journal entries, early timelines of events, police and lab reports, lie detector results, court documents, a mother's personal essay, and lawyers' communications were stuffed into an old leather trunk. It was as if Jay and Jody knew there had to be a reckoning someday. Their truth had to be aired.

"Try to make sense of it," Jay said as he passed me the trunk. "Do the best you can."

Part of the trunk cache was an eighty-page overview of his life that Jay wrote in the early 2000s, while in jail on a domestic charge, in barely legible longhand on loose-leaf paper. Once I learned to decipher what Jay describes as his "chicken scratch," I discovered a deeply compelling personal account. Jay's narrative has been interspersed throughout the book. Those sections—along with his letters from jail to Jody and a number of her diary entries—ground us in the immediacy of Jay's experience and allow a glimpse of how overwhelming it was.

The events and individuals discussed are real, as is their trauma, even all these years later. To protect their privacy but still remind us that they're actual people rather than dehumanized statistics, we've assigned first names to the ten victims of the Hillside Rapist represented in police reports from 1981 and 1982.

Despite one setback after another, all of which can be traced to the brief time he was known as the Hillside Rapist, Jay Chapman has finally stepped forward to tell his story. As he said when we first discussed the project, "It's time."

I sorted through the trunk. I tried to make sense of an insane episode experienced by a seventeen-year-old boy who was blindsided by events so far out of his control that he's wrestled with the *how* and *why* ever since. I emerged on the other side of the process with profound admiration and respect for Jay and Jody's resilience and dogged determination to set the record straight.

—Patrick Coyle, August, 2020

Letter from Jail

Day 3

Dear Jody,

I just got done talking to you on the phone. I picked up your picture and stared at it and started crying, just bawling my eyes out for ten minutes. It hurts so bad that I can't see you and hold you. All I do is cry here. This is my prayer. I say it every day.

> Please, oh Lord, let me get outta this place. Give me the strength to hold on. To see Jody again. She's all I want. She's all I need. I miss her so much. I thank you for bringing her into my life. I want to make a family with her. I know she would be a good wife. Please don't ever take her away from me. She is warm, loving, kind, beautiful, and sweet. Most of all, she has a great figure—best I've ever seen and that's the honest-to-God truth.

That blood test they took has to come back soon. Please pray it does. It has to come back no later than Friday. Please Lord I've got to hear something tomorrow or Friday. Unless they're holding out on it. If they are, they should be fucking punished like I'm being punished. I'm innocent, but some people we both know don't believe that. Please tell them, Jody. Please do that for me, oh Lord. Tell them I'm innocent. I know this is starting to sound like a prayer or something, but that's how I feel right now. I can't stand that people think I did this.

I love you, Jody. I hope I can get on the phone with you one more time before bed to say goodnight. I'm going to get some stuff from the canteen soon. I just borrowed a cig from a guy who wants me to play spades with him. I just lit it up. It's a Kool. I hate Kools. I'm starting to feel a little better. I think it's because I'm writing to you. I'll probably play spades with this guy. I've been reading that book about Jesus that Father Joe brought me. I read how Jesus went around curing people of all kinds of stuff. I dream that could happen to me, but I just don't think it will. Then again, you never know.

My head is stuffed up from all this crying. I feel tired all the time, but I haven't been able to sleep the last two nights. I hear a motor running all night long, and it's a bitch to fall asleep. I think about you all the time. Kissing you. Holding you. Best of all, touching you. Making love to you. Seeing you again will be a dream come true. Please stand by my side at all times because I love you so much. I just saw some lightning flashes. God, I hope they're good luck. I need all the luck I can get right now.

I want to marry you someday, Jody. When the time is right. We will have a baby, and it will be healthy and strong. We will bring it up the right way, with no arguments or nothing. And I won't drink as much as I used to. Just don't drive me to drink. I'm sure that won't happen, because we have a love that is so strong and nobody will ever break it as long as I live. I want to make you the happiest bride that ever lived. I want to buy you the things you want. I want you to have everything you ever dreamed of because you deserve it for standing by me.

It's almost lunch. Tacos today, Jell-O, beans, chips. Nasty. Then I am going to go wait by the phone so I can maybe talk to the one I love. And that's you. So I will end this letter. And start writing another one. Sending a big kiss with all my love now, because later it will smell like tacos.

Love forever and yours always,

Jay

This letter was written by Jay Chapman, eighteen, to his girlfriend of one year, Jody Preimesberger, seventeen. Jay was just beginning a stint at the Ramsey County Jail after being convicted of first-degree rape with a dangerous weapon. His letters to Jody continued on a nearly daily basis for the next month.

1

An Outrageous Violation

Jay Perry Chapman, now fifty-seven, is a handsome, burly blue-collar guy with an infectious laugh, a crinkly smile, and a raspy, Minnesota-accented voice. "I'm no choir boy," he says, absently running his hand through his thick head of salt-and-pepper hair. That's unequivocally true.

He's been drunk and disorderly.

He's been in barroom fights.

He's made terroristic threats to the police. (Never a good idea.)

He's had his driver's license revoked and has driven anyway. Drunk. (Also never a good idea.)

He's been tased by the police during a domestic dispute call. (It took several applications to subdue him.)

He was addicted to methamphetamines for five years, and almost died as a result.

He's been to jail more than once, most recently in

2014 for an aggravated assault; the police report described "great bodily harm" inflicted on the victim. Jay hit a man in the head with a six-foot pump bar used in his siding business, knocking out the victim's teeth and rendering him unconscious until the ambulance and SWAT team arrived. The man was having sex with Jay's nanny (who was also his on-again/off-again girlfriend) in the loft of his garage. Jay was immediately escorted to jail and eventually sentenced to eight months in the workhouse and twenty years probation.

When asked if he would do it again, his answer was immediate: "No. Hell, no. It was the wrong thing to do."

When asked why he did it, Jay said, "I thought she was being raped."

When it was pointed out to him that alcohol appears to have been involved every time he's run afoul of the law, he commented, "It never did much for me."

Jay grew up in Saint Paul's Macalester-Groveland neighborhood, which is considered one of the best places to live in the Twin Cities. It's a place where working-class families live modestly in well-maintained homes alongside urban professionals, artists, and academics who work in the four nearby colleges: University of St. Thomas, Macalester College, St. Catherine University, and Hamline University.

The Mac-Groveland neighborhood extends east from the Mississippi River, with the Union Park neighborhood to the north and Highland Park to the south. On the eastern edge of Mac-Groveland lies the Summit–Cathedral

Hill neighborhood. Summit Avenue, a Saint Paul historic district, is lined with magnificent mansions from the late nineteenth century. Many are now subdivided into apartments and condominiums. At various times, many famous authors made Summit Hill their home: F. Scott Fitzgerald, Sinclair Lewis, Garrison Keillor, and August Wilson.

Grand Avenue, which runs parallel to Summit, boasts bars, restaurants, coffee shops, bookstores, and storefront specialty shops nestled among historic houses. Scenic pedestrian and bicycle trails stretch throughout the neighborhood, in particularly along the Mississippi riverfront.

At the eastern end of Summit Avenue is the Cathedral of Saint Paul, fashioned after the great cathedrals of Europe. It sits on Cathedral Hill and overlooks downtown Saint Paul. Facing the cathedral, across Interstate 94, is the Minnesota state capitol. These two buildings are the architectural pride and joy of Saint Paul.

In the shadows of this great church, a heinous series of crimes began in May 1981 and continued through February 1982. At least sixteen women reported assaults, most resulting in rape, in the streets and alleys of Cathedral Hill during that ten-month period. The crimes were covered in Twin Cities newspapers and the televised evening news for nearly a year. The perpetrator became known as the Hillside Rapist, a name possibly inspired by the well-known Hillside Strangler murders of Los Angeles in the late 1970s.

In the Los Angeles crimes, two cousins were eventually convicted of kidnapping, raping, torturing, and murdering ten women and girls between the ages of twelve and twenty-eight. Both received life sentences without parole.

A few years later in Saint Paul, the victims of another group of assaults gave descriptions of their assailants with some striking commonalities: white male between the ages of sixteen and twenty-four, five feet three to five feet six, one hundred twenty to one hundred sixty pounds, and wearing jeans, a jacket, and a hat with shoulder-length, sandy blond or light brown hair spilling out. Some remembered facial hair, some didn't. Many described facial pockmarks due to acne. They all said the assailant wielded a knife.

The similar descriptions and crimes were enough to lead the Saint Paul police department to believe they were looking for a sole perpetrator, one person responsible for all sixteen assaults and rapes, a serial rapist. Eventually, they concluded that monster was seventeen-year-old Jay Perry Chapman.

Jay had been known to the Saint Paul police for various minor infractions, including truancy, fighting, and theft. When there were drinking parties or other teenage mayhem in the area, it wasn't unusual for Jay to be nearby—or in the middle of the action. He matched the physical description of the rapist. After many months of mounting community pressure to get the rapist off the street, Jay was brought in.

Using a photo, one of the victims of the Hillside Rapist identified Jay as her attacker with "99 percent certainty." This happened many days after the same victim, after looking at Jay in a lineup, stated that "he looked familiar but she could not say for sure."

Four other victims also attending the lineup said he looked familiar, but they couldn't say with any certainty he was their assailant. Then one changed her mind under unknown circumstances. She now stated Jay was the guy, which was enough for the police. They rounded up Jay on a school night from his parents' home on Portland Avenue in Saint Paul and brought him downtown. That was the beginning of what was to become the most nightmarish two months of his life.

Accusations were followed by arrests, releases, follow-up arrests, interrogations, searches and seizures, a weekend on the lam, and, finally, over a month of prison in the adult jail, where Jay was accosted by another prisoner who came to be known as The Big Marine (more about him later.) Finally Jay Chapman, then eighteen, was cleared of the crime by the best forensic science of the day.

But the damage had been done to a young man's psyche, his personal relationships, his opinion of law enforcement, his standing in the community, and his worldview—not to mention the financial status of his working-class parents, who went into debt to cover tens of thousands of dollars for bail and attorney fees.

Jay had one positive constant throughout the ordeal: the love and loyalty of his high school sweetheart and soon-to-be wife, Jody Preimesberger. In an epic example of the sentiment crooned by Tammy Wynette in her 1969 hit, Jody never wavered in standing by her man. She stood by when many in her community, her circle of friends, and even her family believed Jay might have been the rapist. She worked tirelessly through the years to learn more about a criminal justice system that could put a young man—in this case, her young man—through the anguish of living for months as an accused serial rapist on what today seems like flimsy evidence at best.

Jody archived materials and police records and kept journals with an eye toward helping Jay one day write a book to set the record straight. Jody knew how haunted she and Jay were by the false accusations and all that followed. She perceived a connection between the troubled times throughout their marriage and the stretch of time Jay was known as the Hillside Rapist.

Jay wouldn't agree to counseling. He didn't want to relive the painful ordeal with a professional, despite Jody's pleas. In his view, talking about it never helped, it only reopened a deep wound. They both felt writing a book might begin freeing Jay from the past.

All of Jody's work and research was used in the writing of this book.

This is the story of Jay Perry Chapman, who for four excruciating months in 1982 was called the Hillside Rapist. The legacy of those four months has been his shadow ever since.

2

Jay before Jody

My name is Jay Perry Chapman. I was born in 1964 to Jerry and Judee Chapman in Saint Paul, Minnesota. They were great parents, high school sweethearts who eventually married after graduating from Saint Paul Central in 1960. They both worked. My mom, Judee, was employed at Sperry Univac as a printed circuit board assembler. Jerry, my dad, stocked shelves with auto parts for General Trading. It was 1962 when my older brother, Jeff, came along. I arrived in 1964. Five years later, when my little sister, Jolynn, was born, my mom decided to quit her job and become a homemaker. Good thing, too, because seven years later one more would be joining our family, my baby brother, Jamie.

Dad also changed his line of work and became a home remodeler. His specialty was putting new exteriors on old houses with siding, aluminum soffits and fascia, aluminum window wrapping, and new gutters. He became quite successful, and he had a reputation for quality work. His influence on me was profound. I eventually followed him into the same line of work.

Dad worked. Mom raised us. I think my parents were pretty special.

One Christmas morning when we were kids, Dad called to us to get dressed and hurry to the front door. We scrambled into our clothes, shoved our feet into boots, and threw on our jackets. Leading us outside into the freshly fallen snow, he pointed to the ground. "Hey, what do you kids think this is?"

We stared at what could only be sleigh tracks—and boot marks. We were so excited. "Dad! Is that—? Whoa! Santa's sleigh! Look at how deep they go!"

"That's from carrying so many presents," he'd say. "C'mon, let's go see what Santa brought you!" Then he shooed us back inside.

Another Christmas, one of Dad's friends dressed up like Santa and came over to our house. That was such a big deal for us as kids—I'll never forget it.

My parents were committed to each other and the family. That, I think, is what enabled them to get through the hard times and rough patches—and there were plenty of those.

As far back as I can remember we had a motor home, complete with beds and a kitchen, and on the weekends we'd always go out of town. We traveled all over Minnesota and Wisconsin. No worries about where to stay, how much for a hotel for the bunch, or how to feed us. That was all built right into the motor home.

Many other families had a lake cabin up north. We had our motor home. The place we visited most often was the home of my grandparents, Dan and Irene Chapman, on Staples Lake near Comstock, Wisconsin. It was about an hour and a half from the Twin Cities. We always went fishing when we were there. But the lake had too many weeds along the shore for swimming. So as we got older, we'd boat out to the middle and jump in to cool off on a hot summer day. Sometimes we'd drive to a nearby lake that was much cleaner for swimming, water-skiing, and playing water sports.

At my grandparents' lake, we'd poke around in the weeds to find frogs and lift up rocks to search for crayfish—the ones with claws that will pinch you if you aren't careful. We'd also come across water snakes and grass snakes. We dug up worms for bait. My grandfather buried eggshells and coffee grounds in the dirt to attract worms so whenever we turned the dirt over, there would be lots of earthworms and night crawlers. I used to bring in a few six- to seven-pound northerns and walleyes. For me, walleyes were the best-tasting fish. Along the shore, we'd also look for flat rocks to skip across the lake and have contests. We watched those skipping rocks carefully, but sometimes it was hard to count all the skips. So the true winner was often in question.

After having fun beside the lake, we'd explore the woods. Right behind my grandparents' house, about five hundred feet into the woods, was a tree we called the run-up tree because it was at such an angle you could literally run up it.

The woods scared me when I was a kid. I always wanted somebody to go with me until I was about twelve. But I loved running up that tree.

Horseshoe tournaments were a big deal at the cabin. My grandfather was the best at it, often ringing a horseshoe around the stake. That was worth three points. My grandpa was a friendly guy and seemed to know everybody around, so he'd take us to visit his friends. He called the lady friends he knew his girlfriends, but they weren't really. I think he just wanted to get my grandmother jealous.

My grandmother used to worry there wasn't enough activity to keep us kids busy at the lake. If she only knew . . . We were constantly coming up with fun things to do. My grandparents lived right next door to a bar where there was always some kind of action. We often saw people come outside of the bar to settle a score and actually fight. I have to admit, I thought that was cool.

One of my favorite things to do as a kid was to go driving through Saint Paul neighborhoods with my dad.

"Hey, kids," he'd say, "see that house over there, third one from the end of the block?"

Dad would slow down as we all peered out the car windows. We noticed how that house stood out from its neighbors. It'd be shiny, fresh-looking, spiffy.

"Yeah, we see, Dad. What about it?"

"That's one of my jobs. Finished it eight months ago.

Now the neighbor across the street wants me to do their house, so we're driving by to see what kind of job it might be, see what it needs."

I'd study the two houses and wonder what kind of magic my dad did to transform a tired, dreary-looking house into a home that looked so proud of itself. Dad was a skilled carpenter, a pro. He maintained a good reputation, job after job, and became the go-to guy in Saint Paul for exteriors.

I was about eight years old when I started going with my dad to his work sites. When we got to the jobsite, I'd help out a little bit. Then he'd show me where the local park was, I think mainly to get me out of his hair. The parks were usually within a couple of blocks from whatever house he was working on. I'd walk down to the park and play for a while. I'd meet new kids, although sometimes I had a tough time getting along with other kids, especially if there was a bully around. I'd just ignore that type of person. Or if I was getting picked on by more than one kid, I'd leave the park and go back to help my dad.

Being on Dad's jobsites was a huge learning experience for me. I was still young and had to be careful. As I picked my way around the site scattered with tools, stacks of siding, and discarded bits of metal, my dad would watch me. He always reminded me to never walk under the ladder or the scaffolding he was working on. My job was to help pick up the siding scraps and garbage on the ground—hundreds of pieces! Lots of times my older brother Jeff would be helping too. We'd usually get financially rewarded for our efforts.

Dad drove one of the smaller pickup trucks. You can't imagine the equipment he packed on that truck. I was surprised it never flipped over on its side. It was amazing the way he tied down all the materials, ladders, and planks on his work truck. I remember watching him closely when it was time to tie down the motorcycles behind the motorhome along with our pedal bikes. I learned a lot watching him work.

My dad was a stickler about cleaning up his work sites and leaving them neater than he found them. This carried over to our campsites and my grandparents' cabin. Everything was shipshape before we left. I inherited my neatness from both my parents, but my dad was anal about it.

I always looked up to my older brother, Jeff, even though we had our share of arguments. I got his hand-me-downs. My little sister got picked on now and then, but my parents taught me to never pull her hair and never to hit her. My mom was pretty strict about many things, but not picking on my sister was her number one rule. Dad always said, "Listen to your mother, or you'll get a kick in the behind with my work boot." That happened a few times. But was he a good dad. And my mom was a great mom.

On the road, if Jeff and I started horsing around in the back of the motor home, Dad would yell, "Don't make me come back there!" Or sometimes, "If I gotta pull this rig over, you two are gonna get it!" When he said that, we straightened up right away.

Jeff and I had a lot of fun growing up in our neighborhood. There were always lots of other kids to play with. There was a Zenith TV store by the back alley. Whenever they threw away a big box, we'd grab it and bring it to the neighbor's house three doors down. We'd make elaborate forts out of the boxes that kept us entertained for days. The neighbor had lilac bushes all lined up against the fence that ran along the side of his house. We'd actually put the boxes up in the bushes so they were off the ground. Then we'd battle. We filled water balloons and fired them at each other. It was a blast. We all got soaked.

Sidewalk racing was our summer favorite. We had a steel wagon and a fire engine that we took turns driving—or fought over because the wagon was faster. It had bigger wheels than the fire truck and it was lighter. Our friends took turns pushing us to the finish line. After a couple summers, those two push vehicles were pretty smashed up from running into each other.

One of my closest friends growing up was a girl named Debbie. I really liked spending time with her, and I got teased because I played with a girl. The other kids would yell, "Jay has a girlfriend!" I didn't even know what a girlfriend was. I didn't let it bother me too much.

When I was ten, we moved about a mile away to a bigger house with two stories and a three-car garage near Macalester College. We were still in the Mac-Groveland neighborhood, but now we had a bigger house that we all thought was really beautiful.

A couple of years went by before Mom had another son. I was twelve years old. The new guy was named Jamie.

I guess my family is fond of the letter J, that's what all of our first names begin with, starting with my parents, Jerry and Judee. Then their kids: Jeff, Jay, Jolynn, and Jamie. I married a Jody. Our kids are Julia, Jesse, and Justin. Julia's boyfriend is another Jamie. Her children are Jordyn, Jayde, and Jayla. My son Jesse finally bucked the trend by naming his daughter Kaylene, which is only one letter away from J. Close enough, I guess.

When Mom was still in the hospital after Jamie's arrival, I walked over to the florist and purchased some flowers for her and took them to her room. I missed her so much, and I was so happy to see her. "Here, Mom. I brought some flowers for you."

I'll never forget the look on her face.

"Oh, Jay, these are beautiful. What a wonderful surprise. My favorite flowers!"

She reached over and gave me a big kiss. Then she walked me down the hallway to see my new brother. I didn't know what to think. It was amazing. He was such a cute little guy, I thought, compared to some of the other babies in there who looked like extraterrestrials. The nurse brought him back to the room.

"Jay, do you want to hold your little brother?" Mom asked.

"No way. What if I drop him?"

It wasn't long after that I got to do plenty of holding and rocking my brother to sleep. I was the perfect age to babysit him. I listened to everything my mother told me about childcare. I took pride in taking care of my new little brother, and I think I did a good job. My parents must've thought so too because when Christmas rolled around that year there was a little something extra for me in the way of cash.

After my brother was born, I got to have my own room in the basement. I was a teenager now, starting high school, and I needed my own space. My room setup was really cool, with the speakers to my music system situated all around my bed and my prized Hamm's Beer neon sign that came from my grandparents' house shining bright over "the land of sky blue waters."

There was a mirror on my shelf. What did I see when I looked into it? I saw a kid with a pretty normal-looking face, solid jaw, sandy-colored hair, blue-gray eyes—not bad-looking. I liked wearing really worn blue jeans and my comfy jacket. I'd slap a baseball cap on my head, adjust the brim, one more quick look and boom! Out the door. Ready for whatever. And in our neighborhood there was always plenty of *whatever*.

I don't know if it's a good thing or a bad thing but we had a lot more freedom as kids back then. If it wasn't a school day the only rule was get home for meals—otherwise we were on our own. I'll never forget that feeling, from a young age, of not being able to wait until I could get out the door and into the world of people, places, and new experiences. It still hits me—but not like it did when I was a kid.

Mac-Groveland, the middle class neighborhood I grew up in, had a population of roughly twenty-five thousand people at the time. The neighborhood stretches along Summit Avenue to the Cathedral Hill. Summit Avenue, as mentioned, featured huge mansions built by lumber barons who made their fortunes in the Great North Woods of Minnesota. I always thought it was amazing that we lived so close to these magnificent homes.

We used to cruise up and down Summit on our bikes. But we all knew there were certain parts of Summit you didn't cruise alone after dark—mainly the Cathedral Hill neighborhood.

Saint Paul is known for its Irish bars and my family grew up in the shadow of one of its most famous: O'Gara's Bar and Grill on Snelling Avenue. O'Gara's opened in 1941 and officially closed its doors in 2019—seventy-eight years of drinking, storytelling, music, community gatherings, and occasional hell-raising. It's sad that O'Gara's is gone, but there's no shortage of Irish bars in Saint Paul.

Our home was nearby on Hague Street and the bar's parking lot became our playground growing up. My friends and I congregated there to play ball and occasionally climb to the flat roof of O'Gara's garage. Many times when we were horsing around on the roof of O'Gara's, my dad was probably right beneath me having drinks at the long wooden bar where he used to sit with his friends. It was even more likely he was at his usual watering hole, the Trend Bar on nearby University Avenue, about a mile away.

There was always a poodle in our house, and his

or her name was always Andre. I don't remember how many over the years, just that an "Andre the Poodle" was always around.

My father professed himself Catholic by upbringing, but he never went to church. My Lutheran mother sent us to Bible school, because that's what she thought she was supposed to do as a parent. That was the extent of our religious training. We didn't grow up in the kind of strict religious environment that many of my friends did.

My mom kept a perfect house. She passed on to me her obsession for tidiness. I have to have a clean house. If anything is out of place it drives me a little crazy. I'm probably a little anal about that, but it is what it is. That legacy of tidiness carries over to my jobsites too—which definitely comes from my dad, who always kept his work sites impeccable.

My mom cooked one hell of a dinner. Meat, potatoes, and all the fixings; every night there was a meal on the table and we sat down as a family to eat. Her specialty was homemade chicken noodle soup. She made the noodles from scratch.

She was always there to rub lotion on sunburned backs or mend her rough-and-tumble boys when we came home with scrapes, bumps, and bruises—which was pretty much daily. She even fixed me up after I sneaked my beloved go-kart out of the garage once and went joy-riding—against her wishes. She hated that go-kart, and I wasn't supposed to ride it unsupervised. And she was right, it was dangerous.

On this night, well into my nocturnal joyride, I suddenly realized I was being pursued by the police.

I panicked.

Instead of pulling over I put the hammer down and fled. I knew the neighborhood like I knew my own name and my go-kart could go places a cop car couldn't: driveways, backyards, and narrow alleys. Just as I was getting away, my excitement turned to terror when I realized the brakes had stopped working—so I used my feet to stop before crashing into a retaining wall, actually shredding my brand-new pair of tennis shoes. I must have been going pretty fast. It's amazing I survived. My mom was not happy about the shoes.

Another late afternoon, I was riding my go-kart through nearby Macalester College and I noticed a man stapling up signs around campus. The signs were a warning to the public to be on guard for a man who was assaulting people in the neighborhood. The sign had a description on it. I don't remember the assailant's description but I remember being very affected by those signs. *Who would do that?* I wondered. *I hope they get that guy.*

Many nights my dad, Jerry, wasn't home. He traveled the bars after work, which is what a lot of men from my dad's profession did. They worked hard, and they drank hard. This only created a rift in my parents' marriage when money was tight. Then my mom spoke her mind and my dad curtailed his drinking until things got back on track financially. There was no question about it, though; left to his own desires, my dad liked being at the bar with friends—

especially the Trend, where everyone knew his name.

As I got older I worked a lot with my dad and liked it. I was learning about construction, my eventual trade. School was another matter. I didn't like it. I skipped it when I could. I wasn't the brightest kid on the block, so they put me in a special class unit called School Within School (SWS) for kids who had problems in regular classes. I began ditching school a lot and started smoking pot with the other "burnouts" from my class.

When I was about fourteen and in the eighth grade, I was considered kind of a troublemaker in school—the class clown. The principal even had a special room for me in his office, and I would often have to go sit there for hours at a time.

I got into trouble outside of school as well—fights, thefts, stuff like that. It never seemed like a big deal to me until all of a sudden I had to make an appearance in juvenile court, and then another. Before I knew it, I had a police record. I had been to the local police station a few times by now, and the officers and I and we were getting to know each other. I even had my picture taken.

So after my second trip to juvenile court my parents gave me a choice: "You can go stay at your grandparents' cabin this summer or you can go to Boys Totem Town— your choice." Boys Totem Town, which closed permanently in August 2019, was a kind of jail for juveniles. Easy choice. I spent the summer of my fourteenth year with my grandparents, out of the city and away from trouble. I had a great time, and I think it did me some good. When I returned, I had every intention of flying right.

But I fell back into my old behaviors.

Did I mention I started drinking alcohol when I was fourteen? Keg parties happened almost every weekend so access to alcohol was pretty easy. Plus, my dad was a drinker. I think I just assumed that's what males did at a certain age—we started drinking.

My parents were a good couple, but they had their ups and downs. I think the downs were mostly caused by my dad's drinking. I could tell my mom loved him a lot; they had chemistry. He definitely loved her. He'd always say, "Yes, dear" and "I love you, honey." I remember watching my dad walk into the kitchen after dinner, put his arms around my mom and say, "That was delicious, honey." Then he'd give her a big kiss. That meant so much to me, to see how close my parents were.

Then he'd pour himself a drink and eventually fall asleep in his recliner.

Addiction courses through the men in my family, starting with Dad's alcoholism. He was just about a daily drinker when, at forty-eight years old, he shocked us all: he stopped. One day he declared, "That's enough!" And he never drank alcohol again. He's been clean and sober ever since, for thirty years now. At seventy-eight, he's still going strong. I'm sure a lot more pain, struggle, and fear went into his decision to quit drinking than I am making it sound, but he never talked about it—he just did it. Quit drinking. I have a lot of respect for that.

My addiction progressed until I was introduced to

the drug crystal methamphetamine in my thirties, which I began to use almost daily. I call these my "lost years." Not a day goes by that I don't regret picking up that drug, that I don't regret the loss of all that time. The first time I used meth, it was like magic. All the weight I'd been carrying around, the shame and blame and anger and sorrow—it just disappeared. But almost immediately I needed more of the drug for the forgetting to work. Eventually, it stopped working altogether.

I never went looking for drugs, at least not at first. People with the drugs came looking for me because they knew I had dough. I never had a problem working hard and making money, even when I was using, and my drug-using acquaintances knew that about me.

But I'm the one who picked up the drug and used for all those years, and I'm the one who finally said, "No more." I've been free of my addiction to meth for eleven years. I have limited to no contact with old acquaintances who still use, including some family members. That makes me sad sometimes, but I do what I have to do to stay clean. I have just one word to describe an addiction to methamphetamine: insanity.

Before that madness, I had what I'd call a pretty normal upbringing in Saint Paul. We were well provided for by my hardworking father, Jerry, and well taken care of by my strict but loving mother, Judee.

Then in my fifteenth year a wonderful thing happened. I met a girl.

Letter from Jail

Day 5

Good morning, Jody. I love you. It's now four thirty, one half hour before we eat. I was playing spades with a guy today and I won two candy bars. I'll probably lose them back to him later. He's a pretty good player. I've been very depressed, and I'm tired of feeling depressed all the time. I'm just so glad I get to talk to you on the phone. If I didn't get to talk to you, I don't know what I would do. Probably cry all the time. I'm going to supper—then I'll be back. I love you so much. I'm sure you know that by now. I hope you do.

I'm back. It's now six. I'll be taking a shower soon, and I'm wondering if you'll be doing the same? I ate all my supper. We had cheeseburgers with lettuce and tomatoes on them, French fries, strawberry shortcake, and lemonade. We also had coleslaw, but I didn't eat the slaw. Nasty. I'll talk to you after my shower.

I'm back. My hair is dripping wet. My fingers are wrinkled. I love you, my darling. And that's forever. I'm going to go dry my hair and chew the loose skin off around my wrinkled fingers. Gross. Until later.

★ ★ ★

I'm back. My hair is dry. It's six thirty. I'm going to go line up at the phone so I can hopefully get a call in before eight thirty. To my love. That's you. I think you know that by now.

All my love,

Jay

3

Boy Meets Soul Mate

It was a cool, crisp, windy night on January 30, 1980. I was at a party with some buddies, just hanging around being our usual goofy selves—and that's when it happened. A girl walked in. She was with some friends, but the only person I saw was this girl. One look was all it took. I found out her name was Jody. It started with a J. I found out she was fifteen years old. I was sixteen years old. I found out she went to Central High. I went to Central High. It was love at first sight. That sounds cliché, but I can't describe it any other way. I think she felt the same way; that's what I like to think, anyway.

I worked up the nerve to talk to her and I couldn't believe how it easy it was, like we'd known each other for a long time. We just hit it off.

Everything about her just seemed so perfect—her hair, her clothes, her smile, her skin, the smell of her perfume, everything she said, the way she thought about things, the way she treated other people.

I wound up doing exactly what I knew I had to do that night—what I'd never forgive myself for if I didn't—I asked her if I could call her. She said yes and gave me her phone number, and we arranged a time to talk. I floated home on air.

Then I did exactly the wrong thing—I didn't call her at the appointed time. I lost my nerve. I stared at the telephone, picked it up, put it down, stared some more, and decided I wouldn't know what to talk about. *And why would an amazing girl like Jody be interested in a guy like me, anyway?* If I asked her out and she said no, I'd be devastated. I left the house and joined some friends at a party. Turned out there was beer there so I did what many guys before me have tried to do to forget a girl. I started drinking.

Jody waited for my call and when it didn't come she made some phone calls herself. No way was she going to sit home, jilted. Not in her nature. Some of her friends were going to a party and Jody, already dressed for a night out, said she was in. Turns out it was the same party where I was attempting to drink away her memory. When Jody saw me across the crowded room she started walking my way.

I saw her coming and couldn't believe my eyes. She was amazing, more beautiful than I remembered. I just sat there like a deer in headlights, frozen. As she neared, another feeling began to emerge: fear. She was moving fast and there was fire in her eyes. She stepped up, wound up, and slapped me across the face.

"Nobody," she said, "says they are going to call me and then doesn't call."

Then she sashayed back to her shocked but laughing friends. I rubbed my face, which I'm sure was beet red from the slap and embarrassment. I knew immediately that she was the girl for me. For a girl to hit me that hard? She must like me.

I always liked to think of myself as a tough guy but really I'm very softhearted. This girl was tough, and I liked that. That slap was the beginning of an amazing relationship. We started talking and joking and I just kept feeling more and more drawn to her. As the night progressed, we drank keg beer and smoked some pot. We were having a blast. We had so much in common. We went to the same school. We lived in the same neighborhood, but somehow I'd never laid eyes on her before.

We started partying together with friends on the weekends. During the week she'd walk over to my house after school. She felt comfortable hanging out there. We'd find something to do, usually go visit friends in the neighborhood. Soon, we were inseparable.

At night I'd walk her halfway home and give her a kiss good night. She headed south while I went north. I'd walk about twenty paces, stop, and turn around to get my last look at her. I'd walk backwards for a long time, not wanting to lose sight of her before turning around and continuing home. I'd think to myself, *What a great girl—the curves of her body, the sweet smell of her perfume.*

Damn, life is great!

I don't think I've ever been that happy.

Being with her seemed so natural. I had dated a few other girls but nothing came close to the feelings I had almost instantly for this girl. It's like I had been just waiting for her to come along. She was everything I'd ever dreamed of in a girlfriend. No doubt about it, I'd been swept off my feet.

One night, very early in our relationship, we went to a house in our neighborhood, the Hugheses' house, where all the kids hung out—because their parents were almost never around. They were working all the time or something.

Jody and I started to drink alcohol and talk like there was no tomorrow. I never talked to anyone as openly as I talked with Jody that night. I found out about her family. Her dad was a drinking man like mine, and I think she felt comfortable opening up to me about growing up in a dysfunctional home like that. Her mom was kind of a control freak, I guess, sometimes abusive but mainly focused on Jody's sister, Roxy, so Jody kind of operated under her radar.

We consumed a lot of alcohol that night and were feeling pretty buzzed. I glanced at the clock on the wall. It was one thirty in the morning! Jody and I looked at each other—no wonder everybody else in the house had gone to sleep. Still no sign of adults.

She smiled at me, and all my manly instincts started to arise.

"Let's find someplace to crash," she suggested.

"How about upstairs?" I said, looking at the staircase.

"Take off your shoes," she said, "so we don't wake anybody up."

We made it upstairs and noticed a bedroom where there were a couple of beds—but they were all taken. Jody and I turned to go when a girl, asleep in one of the beds, woke up. To my surprise she said, "I'll go sleep with my sister. You guys can have this bed."

There it was—an empty bed. *Oh my God*, I thought to myself. *What do I do now?* I had never been in this position before. I was a fifteen-year-old drunk virgin, getting into bed with the beautiful girl of his dreams.

Our eyes met. I believe she was actually thinking a lot of the same things I was thinking. This was going to be it. We were going to get laid for the first time.

Boy, was I nervous.

After she climbed in, I pulled back the covers. "Go ahead," she whispered. "Lie down."

As I did, I looked at the shape of her body, her beautiful silhouette shaped like a heart. I crawled in beside her. The warmth of her body next to mine was like a furnace. Our bodies touched for the first time. I kissed her lips. It was like magic. The blood in my body was pulsing. The hairs on my arms and the back of my neck were standing at attention. What a sensation. Then my lips were on her neck. She smelled intoxicating. Then her lips were on my neck. *Oh my God*, I thought, *I don't know what she's doing, but please don't ever let it stop.*

Then my hands found their way under her shirt and I touched the flesh of her stomach for the first time. I had never felt anything so soft. I tried to undo her bra but that just wasn't happening. I couldn't figure it out. So she helped me. It just seemed so natural, what we were doing. I tried to take off her pants but couldn't undo the top button. Again she helped me out.

My thoughts were racing. The room was completely black. She couldn't see me. I couldn't see her. She wrapped her arms around my sweltering hot body. Boy, was I excited. And . . . that's as far as it got. My manhood just seemed to burst. Actually being with this girl was more than I could bear. Bam. Over before it really got started. Well, we tried. Close, but no cigar. We held each other in the darkness and eventually fell asleep.

The next morning, we woke. The sun was shining, but the shades were still drawn in the bedroom. We heard people moving around downstairs. Jody and I rolled out, dressed, and walked down to join them. Everyone in the kitchen smiled and looked at us kind of funny. No one had ever looked at me quite like that. Jody and I glanced at each other. We had huge smiles on our faces. Then I saw her neck—she had a big red hickey there. I glanced at myself in a mirror. I had one too. Busted!

"Hey, how was your evening?" one of our friends asked.

"Oh fine, fine," I said. I could feel the red glow of a blush on my face.

We moved into the living room, and I sat in a recliner. Jody came right over to sit on my lap, and I knew she was my girl. I could still smell the sweet aroma of her perfume. She smelled like a wild rose. We sat like that for a while, then got up and said to our friends, "It's time to go. See you guys later."

It was very cold that morning. We had no gloves but we still held hands as long as we could before having to stuff them into our pockets to avoid frostbite. We talked all the way to her house. Then it was time to say our good-byes. We embraced, and I told Jody I'd call her. I walked away with this funny feeling in me. I had really made a connection with this girl. My life was different, and I knew it right away. I got home and this time, I actually called her. We talked on the phone for what seemed like hours, picking up where we left off: likes, dislikes, music, friends. We talked about our parents and she opened up again about her father's alcoholism. I think it was a real problem in their household. Both of our mothers were homemakers. We had so much in common.

I couldn't wait to see her again. "How about tonight?" I asked. "Want to go to a party?"

"It's Saturday, isn't it? Good night to party!"

I told her where to meet me that night. When I saw her, wow, she looked amazing! Even more beautiful than before. This time, it was a garage party. Everyone was drinking beer and having a great time. Jody and I left the party a little early and went to my house. My parents weren't home. They were out at their own party. The living room light was on. Inside, the babysitter my parents hired to watch Jamie sat on the couch.

"Hi, everything OK?" I asked. "Is Jamie upstairs?"

"Yes, he's asleep."

I went to check on my brother who was indeed sound asleep. When I came downstairs, I told the babysitter she could go home.

The house was quiet. Jody and I went downstairs to my bedroom. I put on some soft music and then went upstairs to get some of my dad's vodka. I made a couple of cocktails for us. My parents found out later when they had company over and wanted to make some drinks for themselves—there was almost no vodka left in the bottle. They were really pissed at me and my older brother, so I exercised what seemed like my only option: I blamed it on him. Eventually the truth came out though.

Jody and I started sipping our drinks. We were feeling pretty good. She had on this pretty, button-up blouse. Her hair was done up so nice. I changed albums a few times. Each time I went to sit down, I got closer and closer to her. Finally, I started kissing her, my fingers undoing her shirt. I was doing better this time. Just as I got to the last button, I heard the door of my bedroom open! And there were my parents. Standing there. Staring. They had just arrived home from their night on the town—earlier than I expected! They caught us off guard. My mom snapped on the light. The only light on in the room had been my Hamm's Beer sign. The overhead light instantly changed the mood in the room.

We sat up on the edge of the waterbed.

"Hi, Mom. Hi, Dad. Did you guys have fun tonight?"

"Yeah," answered my dad slowly. I thought I saw him smile. "How 'bout you?"

My mom had consumed a few drinks, which always made her chatty.

"Who is your friend, Jay?" she asked.

"Her name is Jodell, Mom—Jody. We're dating now."

Jody was just sitting there on the edge of the waterbed with her arms crossed, trying to conceal the fact that her blouse had been almost completely unbuttoned. By me. She was embarrassed, but was actually managing pretty well.

My parents sat on the sofa in my room and my mom started rambling on and on, asking Jody questions, telling her all about my childhood. I was embarrassed but not too badly. I was so proud of my mother for the way she acted. She clearly liked Jody, and Jody immediately liked her. Having a few drinks in her probably didn't hurt.

Dad finally left to go check on Jamie. He still had that funny smile on his face. When he returned a few minutes later, he said, "C'mon, Judee, let's leave these kids alone."

"I don't think so," my mom said, still friendly. "Jody, you come upstairs, and we'll make you up a bed on the couch in the living room. OK?"

It's probably a good thing my parents showed up when they did. We hadn't really thought through what was about to happen and I wasn't equipped with protection. The Lord above works in mysterious ways. That was strike two for us. We all turned in for the night.

When we woke the next day, Mom had breakfast on the table. Then I walked Jody home, amazed at how well she'd handled what could have been a really bad situation the night before. She just kept her arms folded over her unbuttoned shirt, her composure intact, the entire time my mother was grilling her—with her shirt unbuttoned!

"See you later," I said, giving her a big kiss. We walked a few paces in opposite directions looking at each other and blowing kisses good-bye. I remember thinking, *She is so special.* You never saw a guy so in love. I walked slowly home, thinking about her the whole way. I entered my house, went straight to my room, put on some music, and started to daydream.

Eventually I jumped in the shower. When I got out, I stood before my mirror. All of a sudden I cared about how I looked. I really wanted this new friend in my life to become my girlfriend. We had so much in common—our attitudes, our ideas, our hopes and dreams. She hit it off with my parents. And I could tell they really liked her. We were like two peas in a pod. I knew she was the one for me—exactly who I wanted, and more.

From that night on, nobody could keep us apart. I had met my soul mate and I was only sixteen years old.

4

Trouble

Jody and Jay joined forces in their sixteenth year and for the next twenty-eight years remained together, a nation of two.

According to Roxy Rutledge, Jody's older sister by one year, Jay was perfect for Jody.

"They had so much in common," said Roxy. "Our families were similar—stay-at-home mom and hard-working, go-to-the-bar dad. Our mother was abusive physically, mentally, and verbally. She had it in for me, but not so much for Jody and Janelle."

Janelle is Jody's twin sister. Jay and Janelle don't have any contact with each other. The past, beginning with the accusations of rape leveled at Jay and all the trouble that caught up with Jay and Jody through the years, strained the relationship to the breaking point.

"It is what it is," Jay says. "Janelle wants nothing to do

with me, and I honor that."

"It was always Jody's dream to settle down and have a family," said Roxy. "From the time she was a little girl, she knew what she wanted. Jay was a guy who could make it come true. He was exactly what she always imagined in a boyfriend, a way out of our dysfunctional family. He worked hard. He partied hard. He treated her well and was very protective of her. He had a skill that would allow them to earn a living. And they had chemistry. She was crazy about him. She met Jay and never looked back—he was her guy."

Jay's lifetime friend from the neighborhood, Tim "Timbo" Reidell, remembers it like this: "Everyone thought they were a great couple. The local police had it in for Jay because he raised a little hell, and he talked a little shit. He wasn't a guy who backed down. But Jody softened him up a little bit. She was always in his corner. You never met a girl more loyal than Jody. Or a guy more in love than Jay. They tried to put all the trouble—what happened to Jay in high school—behind them. But it just finally caught up to them, I think. It was more than they could bear."

Roxy agrees. "Jody always stuck with Jay, through all the trouble. But I don't think they were ever able to completely get past what happened to them when they were still just kids."

Jody and Jay started a family, hell-bent on making a life for each other. And they made it work, keeping their family together and taking good care of their children. But the submerged demons began to take their toll. Jay's drinking escalated. So did Jody's. Then came Jay's introduction to hard drugs.

Methamphetamine is a stimulant that affects the central nervous system, giving a powerful and euphoric high. It swings users from intense pleasure while under the influence to profound depression when the drug's immediate effects fade. While high, users need less sleep and are often more excitable.

Drugs and other chemicals are classified into five categories—Schedules I to V—depending on their accepted medical efficacy and their potential for dependency. Meth is part of Schedule II, a classification that also includes cocaine, morphine, heroin, methadone, oxycodone, fentanyl, aderall and ritalin. Schedule II drugs are controlled because of their potential for abuse and extreme health dangers.

Meth is regarded as one of the world's most addictive substances. It hits the bloodstream and sends a blast of dopamine, the "feel good" chemical, to the brain. To put that in context, sex can lead to dopamine levels of up to 250 units. Cocaine can push dopamine levels to 350 units. With meth, dopamine levels spike to 1,250 units, and the brain creates a hardwired memory of the feeling. But the high doesn't last long. And what goes up must come down in a devastating crash for meth users. The need for more becomes so dire, all other considerations go away.

Addicts describe addiction as a chase for that first high. They're trying to make it "that good" again, which is impossible because repeated use of meth quickly causes the brain chemistry to alter. The natural release of dopamine is blocked. The brain now needs meth to feel pleasure at all, more and more of it over time. Eventually, even that goes away and nothing is left but the dire need to use a drug that is ravaging your mind, body, and soul.

"For a while there," Jay reports, "I didn't care if I lived or died. Jody did drugs toward the end of our marriage too—but not like me. I just wanted to forget, for all the pain to go away." Jody's decline into serious addiction happened after the marriage ended. Her spiral downward was fast, almost without warning. Her main mode of forgetting was vodka.

This is how Jody describes her relationship with Jay in a journal entry written five years before their divorce.

> 1982 started out to be a very good year. We would be graduating from high school, me and my boyfriend of one year, Jay Chapman. There were so many things for a teenager to think about: hopes and dreams, goals in life, starting a family, and no more school—unless you were planning to attend college.
>
> Jay didn't have to worry about that because he was lucky enough to be taught a good trade by his father growing up. All through high school he participated in a work-study program that allowed him to attend school for four hours and then go to work.
>
> Our relationship at the time was really good

and flourishing. Of course we had our ups and downs like all young kids in love do, but I could see myself with this guy for a very long time.

I came from a troubled home life, growing up with an abusive, alcoholic father. So when Jay and I started seeing each other as a couple, it couldn't have happened at a better time for me. I really needed a friend, and God brought me Jay, the man who as the years passed turned out to be my soul mate, lover, best friend, and husband.

We've had our share of trouble, but we always manage to get to the other side of it. I pray we always do.

Jody and Jay were that high school couple who found each other and never looked back.

But on a cold Minnesota night in January 1982—with prom and high school graduation looming, and the girl of Jay's dreams along for the ride—a roadblock to Jay's dream arrived at his parents' front door in the form of two Saint Paul police officers.

"We're here for Jay," one announced to Jay's father.

"He's not here," Jerry told them. "He's out with his girlfriend. I expect him back around ten."

"We'll be back," the officer said. "Tell him not to go anywhere."

"What's this all about?"

"We'll be back."

Jerry sensed it immediately: this was different from

Jay's previous scrapes with the law. The police had been deadly serious. He sat down in the front room and waited for Jay to come home. He had a bad feeling.

Letter from Jail

Day 8

Dear Jody,

I'm so sorry I didn't write you before I went to bed last night. I gave my pencil to Butch, and he forgot to give it back. So I was really bummed out I couldn't write you. I hope you forgive me. I didn't even get up for breakfast I was so bummed out. I can't wait for Father Joe to visit because I know after that you'll be coming to visit me. And I live for that. I'm going back to sleep now. I'll be back to write more after I get up.

Jody, I'm so pissed off right now. Those motherfuckers locked me in my cell for no reason, and now I don't know if I'll be able to talk to you on the phone. I was trying to go back to sleep, and I was under my covers. For *that* I was locked in my cell. What a sad fucking place. This is the sad shit they do to you. I hate the cop who did that. Don't get worried about not talking to me. Please don't. I really want to talk to you. I wrote the sergeant a note. Maybe he'll let me out. I sure hope so. All I can do now is write to you and think about you because you are my darlin' baby forever. Father Joe just arrived and he is coming to talk to me. It'll be great to see him so I can tell him about getting locked in my cell and how much I hate that motherfucking cop.

Father Joe is here. More later.

Yours truly and forever,

Jay

5

Menace

J ody and I attended the same high school, Saint Paul Central. Every morning she walked all the way to my house just to ride the same bus with me. When we arrived at school we hung out with our crowd of friends, chatted, and smoked cigarettes out front until the bell rang.

As I mentioned earlier, I was placed in a special class unit called SWS or School Within School for kids who had problems in regular school. These days they test kids for learning disorders or attention deficits. In my day they popped you into a program that taught you a trade. My summer in the country with my grandparents was supposed to turn me into a better student, but it wasn't working out that way. I continued to ditch classes and smoke pot with the other "burnouts."

That changed when I met Jody. I was into her more than anything, and she was into school. She was a good influence on me. Jody and I would write letters back and forth between classes. We would always go outside and have a cigarette between classes and exchange those letters. She was really into writing those notes. Her penmanship was beautiful. Me, I write like chicken scratch.

Before we knew it, we'd been together for three months, then six months. Life was great. She had a job at Burger Chef on Marshall and Cleveland Avenues. I worked with my dad. Money was tough to find in the winter months, but we managed. I did odd jobs, whatever I could to make ten or twenty dollars so I could go spend it on Jody. I looked forward to seeing her every day.

Then one day I noticed somebody stapling up a public notice with a rendering of a guy's face on it and I flashed back to the first time I had seen someone do this, as a kid on my go cart. Again, it looked like a wanted poster. It had a description of a man on it. They called him a "menace." At the time I didn't pay much attention except to notice that this guy was in my neighborhood assaulting women. I remember thinking, *I sure hope they catch that guy.*

After those posters started going up, I began walking Jody home, all the way up to Five Corners, one block from her house. I thought for sure she'd be safe from there until one night a guy came up to her and exposed himself. *What a pervert*, I thought. *If I ever get my hands on that guy, I'll tear his head off for what he did to my girlfriend.*

We were like glue. Inseparable. Then our lives changed in a really good way. I got a car.

It was a four-door sedan that had been purchased off

the lot by my grandfather, Danny. He drove it for six years and took really good care of it. He then passed it on to my mother, and she drove it for three years before selling it to me when I was sixteen. I took possession of the title in February 1981. I was barely sixteen years old, and I was on fire. I couldn't wait to go pick up Jody and take her for a ride—which I did, that day and every day for the next year, maybe the greatest year of my life.

One of the streets we cruised in my car was Summit Avenue, which cuts through the heart of Saint Paul. As mentioned earlier, it's a famous street, known for its sprawling Victorian mansions. It's almost a tourist destination. But it wasn't always the great street it's considered to be today. Around the Great Depression, the 1930s, it began to decline, hitting its low point in the 1970s and early 1980s, our era. A lot of the grand old mansions were either turned into rooming houses or went vacant.

The area began to slowly turn around again in the 1990s. The Victorian homes became affordable and were restored over time. Neighborhood associations helped with preservation efforts. The Summit Hill District is again a very fashionable place to live in Saint Paul.

But in the early part of the 1980s, when high school kids were joyriding up and down Summit, parts of the neighborhood were considered areas where walking alone after dark was done at your own risk. The James J. Hill House is the biggest, scariest, most imposing mansion along the five-mile stretch. It was built in 1891 by the railroad baron who was called the Empire Builder for overseeing the building of railroad lines through the Upper Midwest, Great Plains, and Pacific Northwest. The Hill mansion is the last before the steep hill that descends into downtown Saint Paul. This is the Cathedral Hill, where the imposing Cathedral of Saint Paul looks out over the city. It's also where the Hillside Rapist conducted his yearlong crime spree. The Hill House is now a museum. We went on field trips there as kids. It's said to be haunted with a chandelier that swings on its own, a spot on a catwalk that produces vertigo, and a ghostly woman in a long black dress who is seen only at night.

We liked cruising this spooky part of Summit the best. The neighborhood is full of dark side streets, winding alleys, secret stairwells, and hidden lanes and pathways that crisscross without rhyme or reason—like a maze. We felt safe as long as we didn't get out of the car.

In early February 1982, Jody and I were out on a school night, which meant I'd have to be home by ten or ten thirty. I dropped Jody off at her house, and I went home like usual.

That was the last joyride we would ever take.

6

First Arrest

My dad was waiting up for me.

Something was wrong. He never waited up. No one did—I usually went straight to my room. Everyone else was always in bed.

"Jay," my dad said, dead serious. "The police were here earlier this evening."

"For what?" I asked.

"They said you assaulted a woman."

I felt shock. I tried to think. Usually when the cops said I had done something, I had done something. But assault? *No.*

"Dad, I didn't."

The only thing I could think of even coming close to an assault was a disagreement I had with Jody a week or two earlier.

"They said they'll be back to question you. Tonight."

I was stunned. Before I could respond there was a loud knock on the door. Clearly, they'd been waiting for me. Two Saint Paul police officers entered our home—one young, one older. I thought, *No problem. I didn't do anything wrong.*

The older cop asked me one question: "Did you assault anyone lately?"

"No," I said.

I could tell they didn't believe me. We stood there, awkward, in kind of a standoff. They asked me again to tell them about an assault that had happened in the Hillside neighborhood and I said, "I don't know anything about that."

Then my dad asked if he could have a private moment with me.

After some hesitation they allowed it.

He took me through the kitchen and into the dining room. He shut the door. He looked me in the eye and asked me point-blank, "Do you know anything about this, Jay? Did you assault anyone? I want the truth."

My exact words: "Dad, no. Jody and I got into a disagreement about a week ago. I raised my voice."

"I don't think that's what they're here about."

"Then I have no idea what they're talking about."

That was enough for my dad. "Let's go. Cooperate fully, and tell the truth."

The police arrested me that night. In my parents' living room. They read me my Miranda warning, placed me in handcuffs, and said, "You're going downtown." I'll never forget the look of horror on my mom's face as they led me out to their squad car.

When I decided to write this book, I asked Mom if she'd be willing to jot down some notes about her memory of what happened to me in my eighteenth year. She returned the next day with a typewritten essay, "A Mother's Perspective." I get a little emotional when I read it because I can hear my mother's voice so clearly every time. Here's how my mom describes the events of the evening the police arrested her son on a charge of rape:

> We were quietly watching television. It was around seven o'clock when there was a knock on the door. It was the Saint Paul police asking for my son. He was not home, but was due back at ten thirty. My husband asked what they wanted him for. They were quite evasive but said it had to do with a sexual assault. He was wanted for questioning. My heart started pounding. What could they possibly be talking about? My son wanted for a sex crime? That couldn't be. He had a nice girlfriend, and he spent all his evenings with her. He wasn't the kind of boy who would commit a sexual assault.
>
> He had his own car at this time. We told the police what kind of car it was and when he'd be home. He had no sooner arrived and the police were back again to pick him up. He was handcuffed and brought to the juvenile detention

center. Before he left, my husband took Jay aside and asked him if he was guilty of this crime. He said, "No, Dad!" That was enough for me to believe my son had not committed the horrendous crime he was being accused of. But that night was just the beginning of the nightmare.

In 2016 my mom, Judee, died tragically of amyotrophic lateral sclerosis (ALS), a brutal, unforgiving disease. I still miss her every day. So does the rest of my family. She was our heart and soul. My dad, who took exceptional care of her until the very end, can't mention her without getting emotional. She never wavered in her belief in my innocence. Neither did my dad. That means the world to me.

My dad's parting words as the cops were hauling me out the door that night were: "Tell the truth, you have nothing to hide."

That's exactly what I intended to do.

At the juvenile detention center the police led me directly to an interview room and began questioning me.

"Tell us about the assault."

"What assault?" I immediately told them about the argument I had with Jody that had resulted in raised voices. "But we patched it all up."

The questioning took an immediate, aggressive turn. "You're going to tell us about the fucking assault, Jay, and we're waiting right here until you do."

This was insane. This was serious. I insisted I had

nothing to tell them about any assault.

The interrogators would occasionally leave the room and then return.

"Tell us about the assault, Jay."

"I don't know anything about it."

It was getting late. I'd been there for hours. I was scared, hungry, and tired. I thought about my dad, probably waiting for me in a room somewhere outside. Eventually I asked when I would be able to go home.

"You're not going home," they said.

I was led into another room in the juvenile detention center with a cot and they locked the door. *What a nightmare. They really think I'm the guy.*

The next day the interrogation became more intense. Occasionally a police officer tried a softer approach. They wanted a confession, and it didn't seem like they were going to let me leave until I gave them one. Eventually I clammed up altogether and said nothing. *I'm not the guy who committed this crime. They don't seem to want to accept that, so I'm not saying another word.*

Then I learned something shocking—a ten-thousand-dollar bail had been put on my head. Not only was I a suspect, I was the *only* suspect.

"We've been gathering information from the victims for months," the police told my father.

"Victims?" my dad asked. "More than one?"

"Sixteen," said the police. "Ten have filed charges. They all described the same guy, and we believe it's your son."

They were calling me a serial rapist.

My father went to the bank and borrowed money to get me out. *I'm going to owe him for the rest of my life.*

He also contacted an attorney. I knew my dad would only do that if he thought there was serious trouble.

The last thing the police said to me before I was released was pretty ominous: "Don't go anywhere, Jay," they said. "We're gonna be in touch."

We left and the first thing I did when I got home was call Jody. I told her everything that had happened from the last time I saw her. She was very quiet as she listened. Then she said three things to me I'll never forget.

1. "I believe you, Jay."

2. "I can prove it." (I asked how.)

3. "My diary."

I didn't know Jody had a diary and that she'd been documenting just about our every move for the past year. She offered the diary to the lawyer. Jody is a private person. I know what it cost her to turn over her diary like that.

7

Serial Rape

The term *serial rapist* was coined in 1974 by Federal Bureau of Investigation (FBI) profiler Robert K. Ressler to describe offenders who are obsessed with "fantasies that go unfulfilled," pressing them onward to the next offense.

Serial rape is defined by the FBI as two or more related cases involving rape or sexual assault behavior.

In Saint Paul, Minnesota, the number of assaults and rapes on women in 1982, the year of the Hillside Rapist, spiked a shocking 40 percent, even while other violent crimes that year, like homicide, saw a significant decline.

In 1981, according to a study conducted by Ramsey County Medical Center, of the 200 rape victims they saw, only 5 percent wound up in court. Still, the Saint Paul police department reported having solved 47 percent of the rape cases that year.

In an article published by the *Saint Paul Pioneer Press*

in August 1982, Lieutenant Larry McDonald, then head of the sex crimes unit, explained why he thought the number of cases landing in court was so low. "Most rapists work alone. Unlike other crimes, there is no accomplice to snitch to police. The rapist rarely takes anything or leaves anything that can be traced back to him. There are rarely witnesses to rapes, and investigations can take months. By that time, the victim often wants to just forget the crime and stops cooperating with police."

McDonald then gets to what he believes is at the heart of the matter: "But even if a woman takes the case to court, the suspect will often admit to having sex but will claim she consented. A jury then has to decide who is telling the truth."

At the time, the Violence Against Women Act of 1994 (VAWA) was ten years away from being enacted. VAWA created rape shield laws to protect women against hostile questioning by a defense attorney. Before then it was commonplace to grill victims on the stand about what they were wearing, if they'd been drinking, how many sexual partners they'd had in the past—everything a defense attorney could think of to paint the victim in a bad or supposedly promiscuous light.

Rape shield laws now limit the ability of a defense lawyer to introduce evidence or question rape complainants about their past sexual behavior. Today's rape shield laws also prohibit the publication of the identity of an alleged rape victim. These protections haven't stopped unfair, blistering defense attorney cross-examinations, but precedent laws now reign in prosecuting attorneys and judges from allowing this type of questioning.

The sad truth is that many women, after enduring the trauma of rape, can't bear the thought of having to relive it in court, in front of the alleged perpetrator, considering the possibility they won't be believed or will be depicted as deserving of the assault in some way.

In 2006 a small, quiet movement was started in Chicago by social activist and community organizer Tarana Burke, to promote "empowerment through empathy" among women of color who had been sexually abused. It sprang from an interview she was having with a thirteen-year-old girl who confided in her that she had been assaulted. Burke wanted to provide comfort by responding "me too" because she had also been the victim of an assault. But she didn't and later regretted not sharing her trauma with a fellow victim. So she began the Me Too movement in her community.

Me Too blew up in 2017 after the arrest of movie mogul Harvey Weinstein on assault and rape charges. A long list of Weinstein's accusers began to come forward. On October 15, 2017, actor Alyssa Milano took her experience to the social media platform Twitter, suggesting that if other sexual assault victims would reply to her tweet with "Me Too," the enormity of the problem might be revealed. Within twenty-four hours the hashtag #MeToo, with its origins in Burke's social activism and organizing, had been retweeted or reposted twelve million times. A movement was born across the world.

8

Court

My father took it upon himself to find a lawyer. I knew he was adept at troubleshooting problems at work, but he stepped up and showed me how good he was at handling a personal crisis. I didn't care for the lawyer. He seemed mostly interested in getting paid. We went downtown to his office, where we were informed he needed a twenty-five-hundred-dollar retainer to get started. So my father wrote a check. I couldn't imagine the strain this was putting on my parents. I knew my dad hated forking over money for a crime I didn't commit. The lawyer said he'd let us know when a court date was set.

"What do we do in the meantime?" Dad asked.

"Keep your nose clean."

Like I said, I never really liked him.

The court date arrived. It was to be held in juvenile court because I was still seventeen. My dad had a nice suit in his closet. He took it off the hanger and laid it on the bed. I remember looking at it and thinking, *That's a fine-looking suit.*

"Try this on, Jay."

It was a little big, but it looked pretty good. My mother adjusted the collar, picked at the shoulders a little bit, and said, "This will be fine."

My father opened the drawer of his dresser and pulled out a little box. Inside were gold cuff links. He helped me put them through the holes on the French cuffs of my fancy shirt. Mom fixed my hair. Dad brought me some shoes to wear. I stood back and looked in the mirror. *Damn*, I thought, *I've never looked so good in my life.* All to go to court. It still didn't hit me what was about to happen.

As we were driving to the courthouse, my dad was telling me how to behave. "Act proper. Stand and sit up straight. Look professional." I was trying to concentrate on what he was saying, but I was pretty distracted. I checked myself in the car mirror. Clean. I'd cut off all my long hair. I hardly recognized myself.

We walked into the courthouse building. Our lawyer wasn't there yet, so we waited for him in the lobby. I was about as nervous as I'd ever been. Eventually the lawyer showed up with a shiny briefcase and said, "Follow me."

He took us into another room, where he told me the person I allegedly assaulted would be in the courtroom. "Whatever you do—do not stare at her." Then he started talking to my dad, and I looked out the window. This was the same building I'd been in for questioning. I was looking at the same view I had from my jail cell two weeks prior. I could see Church of the Assumption, a beautiful old Catholic church on West Seventh Street. Built just after the Civil War, it's the oldest church in Minnesota. *They sure built that church to last*, I thought. Constructed out of gray Mississippi River limestone, the church had a big clock on all four sides of its steeple. I stood there just gazing at it, marveling at it. I guess my mind needed something to focus on besides what was about to happen.

Then they called my name. We entered the courtroom and sat down at a huge table. The judge's bench was right in front of us. The room was circular. Off to my left were some other tables. The empty jury box was on my right. The palms of my hands were moist. I was getting progressively more nervous. Then the judge entered. Everybody stood. Now my armpits were dripping with sweat. Next to the judge's bench and behind a table was a lady, approximately fifty years old.

Everybody sat down, and with a bang of the gavel, the court was in session.

The lawyers were talking, but I couldn't concentrate because it suddenly dawned on me that I was being accused of raping this woman—this small, fifty-something-year-old woman sitting behind another table. I was shocked and humiliated when it sunk in that some people in the room thought I was the guy who did that. I wouldn't even think about that with a woman her age. I wasn't even out of high school yet. It was my senior year, and I was dating a beautiful girl and deeply in love with her. She was all I wanted in a woman. How could they think I did this?

They said I looked just like the guy all the victims described. He wore a baseball hat and used a knife. I often wore a baseball hat. In fact, I had a baseball hat collection. I worked at fairs for a couple of years with my Uncle John. I used to travel to Milwaukee, Wisconsin, and work for ten days at the Wisconsin State Fair and then ride the Royal American Shows train to Saint Paul to work the Minnesota State Fair. I was a ring boy, the kid who collected the rings fairgoers tried to toss around Coke bottles to win a prize. We had the biggest stuffed animal on the Midway. I saved all my Royal American Shows hats. One from the Wisconsin State Fair was my favorite.

They were also saying the perpetrator was between the ages of sixteen and twenty-five, stood about five three to five six, weighed about a hundred fifty pounds, and had dishwater-blond hair.

And when asked, the fifty-year-old woman looked at me and said, "Yes, I believe he is the guy who did it."

I wanted to die when I heard her say that.

The prosecuting attorney handed my lawyer a stack of papers that he eventually passed on to me. In that stack of papers was a picture of a human body with arrows pointing at it. It said something about secretions. I didn't know what that meant at the time. According to the reports in the stack of documents, the perpetrator penetrated the woman with his penis. He had sexual intercourse with her. He forced himself on this poor lady. He put his penis in her anus and ejaculated, so she had to get "scraped" at the hospital for evidence to be used in a test later.

I couldn't read any more.

We left the courtroom. In the hallway, my attorney asked for more money. My father had no choice but to pay him another twenty-five-hundred dollars. We left the courthouse and proceeded to go home. I lay on my bed and stared at the ceiling.

I was getting close to my eighteenth birthday. That meant I was about to be treated as an adult by the court system.

All I could think about was that for almost a year some guy had been hunting down women to rape them, and there were people who thought it was me.

Then I had another thought: *prom*. Jody and I were supposed to go. Should I cancel? Jody would be very disappointed if I did that.

The hell with it. We're going. I'm not who they say I am, and I'm going to act accordingly.

9

Prom

Central High's 1982 prom was held at Town Square in downtown Saint Paul. I bought myself a brand-new pair of shoes. My mother took me up into the attic and opened an old trunk. Inside, to my surprise, was a tuxedo with tails. It was old and needed some alterations, but it was nice. Mom fixed it all up for me. Damn, did I love her for doing that. She really cared about how I looked. Especially at that time, with rumors flying and people talking about me. Word of my arrest had slipped out.

I polished my new shoes, had the suit dry-cleaned, and bought a new white shirt at Montgomery Ward in Midway Shopping Center, the same store where I usually did all my Christmas shopping. Jody told me she bought a new dress.

The night arrived. I showered, dressed in my suit with tails, and drove to my love's house. I think even her parents were impressed by the way I looked. I always had this feeling they didn't care for me much because I had a bad-boy reputation around the neighborhood. Given the latest development, I was nervous about even going over there, but Jody said it would be OK.

Her mom greeted me and told me to have a seat on the couch. Before long, I heard a noise from the top of the stairs and suddenly, there was Jody in a blue dress. She was just so beautiful. Took my breath away. How did I ever end up with such an amazing girl? As she walked down the stairs, I watched her every move. My heart was pounding so loudly I was afraid her parents could hear it.

I gave Jody the corsage I'd picked up at A. Johnson & Sons Florist, the same florist I went to when my mom had my little brother Jamie and I brought her flowers. The corsage cost me fifteen dollars. That was a lot of money in those days.

She smelled so good. I wanted to wrap her in my arms, but instead I just gave her a little kiss. She went to her refrigerator and brought back a boutonniere for me. She tried to pin it on my lapel. I could tell she was nervous. We both were. Her mom stepped in and helped. Then her mother got out the camera and she took half a dozen pictures.

Her father didn't say much. He stayed in the kitchen, drinking his coffee. As we were about to leave and return to my house so my parents could take pictures, Jody's mom stopped us: "You kids have a nice time. You hear? I mean it."

It was almost a warning. Like this might be the last night of fun you're going to have, so make it count.

I told her we'd have fun and that her daughter was in good hands with me.

We proceeded out of the house, Jody's arm wrapped in mine. We got to the car and I opened Jody's door to let her in. I wanted to be as polite and grown up as possible— I knew her mother was watching. I jumped in, closed the door and the tail of my suit got caught in the door so I had to open it and free my suit. I made sure that didn't happen again for the rest of the night.

We continued to my house. I could see my parents looking out the front window when we arrived. Ever the gentleman, I got out of the car first, went around and opened Jody's door. We went inside so my mother could take more pictures.

As we were about to leave, my father slipped me a twenty-dollar bill and said, "Have fun." That extra money paid for dinner at O'Gara's Bar and Grill. I always remembered how good the food smelled when we played in O'Gara's parking lot as kids. I finally had the money to eat there.

After dinner we went to prom. We stayed for a couple of hours and kept our promise to Jody's mom—we had a lot of fun. Boy, did my date look fine. She looked like a model. We danced and socialized, and then we left downtown and drove our regular cruise up Summit Avenue to Mississippi River Boulevard. We parked at our secret hangout, a place called Hidden Falls. We made out a little, and then went to my house.

My parents told me to be home at twelve fifteen because I had borrowed their car. We were there on time. I drank no alcohol earlier that evening. I saved it for after I was done driving. My mom said that was the rule: we could have a drink once we got back to the house, and not before. I agreed.

While Jody sat on the couch in my bedroom, I broke open a bottle of wine. She looked so innocent. I took more pictures of her. I couldn't get over how beautiful she looked.

It seemed like we talked for hours. Before we knew it, we were lying in bed, holding each other tightly. We drifted off to sleep. I had such sweet dreams that evening. We spent the whole night like that. My mom didn't even come downstairs to tell Jody to sleep on the couch. They must have known we were in love. Maybe my mother finally listened to my father when he said, "Aw, just leave them alone."

I'll never forget that night. For an entire evening, I never once thought about the trouble occurring with the police. I was in the arms of my love during what might have been the last carefree night of my life.

10

Victims

When we decided to write a book, Jody took her job as researcher seriously. She was planning a trip to the police department to get copies of the police reports relating to the case of the Hillside Rapist when my mom told her, "You don't need to do that."

Turns out my mother had privately asked our lawyer for those the day I was released from jail. He made copies of every police report for her, and she filed them away in a manila envelope that went untouched for a couple decades. My mom saved everything that had anything to do with her family: the good, the bad, and the ugly.

The following descriptions of the activity of the Hillside Rapist come directly from those reports. Careful consideration has been made to protect the identity of the victims. We decided to include these descriptions of the crimes to provide the full scope of what I stood accused of and, more importantly, to not minimize the horror of what the victims of sexual assault endure.

I tried to read the police reports when Jody first got her hands on them from my mother. I discovered I can't do it. They've been in my possession, unread, for almost two decades.

I can't bring myself to read them—but I can't bring myself to throw them away either. These represent accounts of victims who agreed to provide statements to law enforcement. The police knew about at least six others, possibly more.

The police reports, loosely stacked in a dog-eared manila envelope at the bottom of the trunk, were in surprisingly good condition for being almost forty years old. They're written in terse, just-the-facts language that starkly contrasts with the events being described. Typos are x-ed out or covered with white-out solution. The reports are all numbered and focus on exact times, dates, and locations. Data.

When reading the dry recitation of facts, page after page, it can be challenging to remember that at the center of these stories, told without embellishment, are human beings who were the victims of an outrageous violation. We're not using the victims' actual names—out of respect and concern for their privacy. But we have decided to assign invented names to honor and humanize them.

Ellen

On Sunday morning, May 17, 1981, at around 2:30 a.m., Ellen was asleep when a man crawled into her second-story Cathedral Hill apartment window and raped her at knife-point. He had removed a screen window to gain access.

Ellen, who was in her thirties, was married, but her husband was out of town on a business trip. He was due back the next morning. She'd been at a friend's that evening, "listening to music, eating food, talking, drinking wine." She had two glasses and was home shortly after midnight. She noticed a "big silver vehicle" in her husband's parking spot, but nothing else was out of the ordinary. She went to bed. When she awoke to a man crawling on top of her she thought, for a split second, it was her husband.

The ordeal lasted fifteen harrowing minutes, during which the rapist said four things:

"What's your name?"
"You can call me Pat."
Then later: "Did you enjoy it?"
"Was I good?"

The knife he used was a butcher knife. Ellen was brought to the hospital. There she described her assailant as a "white male, five foot six, one hundred fifty pounds, medium build, wearing a ball cap with light brown hair spilling out, a blue jacket or sweatshirt, approximately twenty-one years old."

Her husband returned home early that morning and went straight to the hospital. Ellen was still shaking, unable to stop crying.

The police eventually drove them both home. According to the police report, "They held each other in the back seat of the cruiser and were silent."

Sarah

The next assault occurred less than two weeks later. Same neighborhood. The circumstances and the description of the perpetrator led police to strongly suspect they were dealing with the same criminal.

The rapist's first assault seemed to have emboldened him. He found what he wanted and in the middle of the night broke into a home and took it. His second assault had a very different result.

A man forced his way into the Cathedral Hill apartment of Sarah, a single woman, around 3 a.m. on May 30, 1981. Sarah had been awakened by sounds outside her house. When she opened her screen door to investigate, a man leaped over the railing. She slammed her sliding door shut but the man smashed into it, derailing it from its sliding track.

He grabbed Sarah and put his hand over her mouth while she struggled. He attempted to begin this assault the same as the last one, by inviting her to call him by a first name. "You can call me Marty," he said.

The victim bit him. Hard as she could. He yanked his hand away, and she screamed, "You son of a bitch!" She repeatedly screamed these words while her assailant attempted to overpower her. She clawed his hands and face, leaving her with several broken nails. She kicked. She spit. She fought back like a trapped animal and never stopped screaming.

Her assailant eventually turned and fled out the screen door, leaping over the railing and running away.

Sarah watched him go and reported that he looked back at her three times. Asked if she thought she'd be able to identify her victim, she said, "Hell, yes."

The rapist had met his match in Sarah. She prevented him from raping her.

Women are often told that if they're attacked and have the chance they should fight back. That's not always easy, or even possible, when surprised and overcome by an attacker. Not that there's universal agreement on the wisdom of that strategy.

Statistics show that if women fight back, their odds of being raped are cut in half, while their odds of being injured are raised by 10 percent. The main thing is to live through the assault.

The husband of Ellen, the first victim, is mentioned in the police report. Most partners of rape victims report great difficulty dealing with feelings of shame, rage, hurt, and powerlessness. Many relationships don't survive the aftermath of a sexual crime. Months later, Ellen's husband told a reporter he knew where the accused rapist (Jay Chapman) lived and stated his intention to find him and kill him. No attempt on Jay's life was ever made but he, Jody, and the entire Chapman family lived in fear of retribution for a long time.

"I never blamed Ellen's husband for that threat," Jay says. "If someone raped Jody, that would have been my reaction too."

The neighborhood hoped and prayed the attacks were over. So did the Saint Paul police department, which had been under mounting pressure to get this criminal off the streets and keep one of their most densely populated communities safe.

Had the rapist been scared straight by Sarah, who fought back? Had he come to his senses, changed his ways, realized he was dealing with human beings and not animals?

A community held its breath and attempted to go back to living their lives without the specter of a violent neighborhood rapist.

Letter from Jail

Day 13

To the girl I love, and that's you, my dear. I'm sure you know that by now . . . One more day, waiting on the court to see what they say. I hope it goes the way I want it to.

They should at least lower the bail or drop it. If they don't, I guess I'll just sit here for who knows how long.

I pray to get out of here. So I can tell you how much I love you. So I can tell you how much I miss being with you. I miss that the most, holding you in my arms and making love to you. I feel really lonely right now.

There are a few guys here who think they're pretty bad. They'll get what's coming to them. I try really hard to get along with them but there always have to be a couple assholes in the crowd.

The train just came by, the Amtrak. It comes past every night at ten. I wait for it. I dream I'm on it, with you, getting away from here instead of being locked up in this fucking jail. I'm going to bed now, so I can think about how much I love you and how much I can't wait to make love to you again.

Good night, my love,

Jay

11

Jody's Diary

Jody went shopping with her twin sister, Janelle, one day in early 1981—after we met, after she slapped me across the face for not calling her on the phone. She made a purchase, the kind of purchase just about every teenage girl made before social media. Maybe they still do, I don't know.

She bought a diary.

Jody loved to write. Letters. Cards. Notes. Diary entries. About what she had for breakfast. What song was playing on the radio. What someone said to her at school or at her job at Burger Chef. She was kind of anal about recording the times and dates of everything.

She made an entry just about every day, even if it was just a couple words. Her diary sheds so much light on our comings and goings in 1981, one can only imagine it played a major role in the work of the Saint Paul police department as they investigated the case of the Hillside Rapist.

Right?

That's not what happened.

The date of the first rape was the day of our prom— which Jody and I attended, of course. And which Jody wrote about in her diary, of course. According to the details in her diary, it would have been difficult for me to pull off the crime.

Same with the second rape. We'd been traveling that weekend, to my grandparents' place in Wisconsin. Jody wrote about that too. I'll let her tell you about it.

The inside cover of Jody's diary has an inscription:

This diary is the property of Jody Preimesberger.
The only other person allowed to read this diary,
besides myself, is Jay P. Chapman.

Jody would approve that we're peeking into her diary for the purposes of this book and proving my innocence. Only pertinent passages are included.

Jody turned over her diaries to Jay's lawyer, who passed them on to the Saint Paul police department. Whether or not the investigators ever read the diaries and compared Jody's account of their activities with the dates and times of the crimes is unknown. The diary contains relevant information that was either not noticed or was discounted by investigators anxious to assuage an outraged community and make an arrest.

The first entry in sixteen-year-old Jody's new diary is succinct:

January 30, 1981
Met Jay Chapman!

The next few entries similarly reflect a young couple falling quickly, madly, deeply in love. This next entry comments on the night Jay didn't call Jody as planned, and then they both ended up at the same party. It was a scene straight out of a rom-com—the night that began with a slap across the face and ended with a first kiss.

January 31, 1981
Was at Pat S.'s party. So was Mister Jay
Chapman!!!

February 2, 1981
Dad's forty-fourth birthday. Talked to Jay
Chapman on the phone! He is very easy
to talk to. I like his voice. We have a lot
in common!

February 3, 1981
Saw Jay Chapman again!

February 4, 1981
Saw Jay today. [Smiley face.]

February 5, 1981

Met up with Jay Chapman. He asked me
out to dinner for his birthday. I said . . . yes!

February 7, 1981

Jay's seventeenth birthday. We went to
the Red Lobster together. I ate shrimp. It
was sooo good!!! Had a *really* good time.
[Smiley face.]

February 15, 1981

Started taking the pill.

The next few weeks are filled with the daily minutiae of
a Minnesota teenager attending high school, going steady
with a boy, and otherwise living her life. There are entries
about shopping, attending Saint Paul's Saint Patrick's Day
Parade, and going on dates with Jay Chapman. According
to her diary, Jody and Jay saw the movie *Fame* on May 24,
1981. She loved the widely anticipated film about the lives
and hardships of performing-arts high school kids from
New York trying to make a name for themselves. She could
relate to it. She was trying to make a name for herself, trying to carve out a future with the boy she had fallen for, a
future she felt very optimistic about at the time.

Other entries touch on going to work at Burger Chef,
hanging out with girlfriends and her sisters, avoiding her
father, arguing with her mother—pretty usual stuff.

From May 15 through June 1, 1981, seventeen days in

Jody Preimesberger's sixteenth year, a handful of innocu-
ous entries shed pertinent light on the case of the Hillside
Rapist. Jay was with Jody at times and places that would
have made it nearly impossible for him to be the rapist.

May 15, 1981
Worked. Prom tomorrow!

May 16, 1981
Prom day. Prom is 8:00 p.m. to 12:00 a.m.

Picked up flowers at 3:00 p.m. They cost
$3.64.

Went to prom. Slept over at Jay's. Had a
really good time.

[Smiley face.]

May 17, 1981
Got home from prom at noon the next day.

According to Jody, she and Jay went to their prom on
the evening of May 16 and were together the entire night.
When the prom ended at midnight, they left together and
went to the Chapman house. At some point, relatively
soon after arriving at the Chapmans' house, Jody and Jay
fell asleep. It's where they both woke up the next morning.
In each other's arms.

According to the police, though, Jay wasn't with his
girlfriend in the early morning hours after prom. They

alleged he was breaking into a Cathedral Hill apartment and holding a woman hostage before raping her. Adding travel time from the Chapman house to the apartment to the length of that attack, Jay would've had to sneak out for forty-five minutes to an hour.

Is it possible Jay slipped out that night, unbeknownst to his parents and his girlfriend, from about 2 to 3 a.m. to commit this crime? It's not very likely, but it's possible.

Here are other entries with noteworthy connections to the case against Jay:

May 28, 1981
Roxy's birthday. Did NOT go to school.

May 29, 1981
Going with Jay's family to Chapmans' cabin in Wisconsin for the weekend! Can't wait.

May 30, 1981
At the Chapmans' cabin. Having a good time. Four months going (steady) with my baby, Jay.

May 31, 1981
Had so much fun at the Chapmans' cabin this weekend.

June 1, 1981
Pay day. $100. Jay and I got in a big fight.

> I went to work from 1:30 to 6:00. I went
> shopping and got new pants and a shirt.
> Ate dinner at York Steak House. Still upset
> about that fight.

According to Jody, on Friday, May 29, they were traveling to the cabin of Jay's grandparents, which was close to Comstock, Wisconsin, and arrived without incident. On Saturday, May 30, they spent the day and night there and "had a lot of fun." On May 30, they traveled back to Saint Paul.

According to investigators, though, Jay slipped away from the cabin to drive the eighty-one miles from Comstock to Saint Paul—a ninety-minute drive. Then, they accused, he broke into an apartment and attempted to rape a woman who fought him off by biting his hand and clawing his face (as evidenced by her broken, bloody fingernails) before returning to the cabin. If so, his absence went unnoticed by Jody, who records in her diary that they spend a "fun" day together.

Possible? Yes, barely. Probable? No.

It appears unlikely that Jody's diary entries were given significant, if any, consideration by the Saint Paul police department as they held Jay in jail on serial rape charges. No one from the department ever followed up with Jody, Jay, or any member of either family about her diary entries—suggesting they were summarily ignored. Now, almost four decades later, it seems obvious how the police could've used the details in her diary to rule out Jay as a suspect. Their mistaken certainty that Jay was the perpetrator kept them from continuing to investigate the attacks thoroughly.

In May and June 1981, as Jody quietly chronicled her days, the Hillside Rapist was just getting started.

Letter from Jail

Day 19

Jody,

It's 7:30. I'm in lockdown for twenty-four hours. That's what they do if you get in a fight. I'm scared. Tomorrow they'll be moving me, and I pray to God I'm going to get along with the people in the new pod. This place is so bad. This place really sucks. Oh my God, I hope my dad gets me outta here. Soon. Tomorrow. I pray to God. I'm going to be fucked if he doesn't get me out of here. I'm starting to not care if I get the shit beat out of me or not—that's how bad it's getting.

I have a little better scenery out the window of my new cell. I see the Schmidt Brewery. Damn does that sound good right now, a nice cold bottle of beer. And a joint. And you.

I'm going to try to get some sleep. I love you so much, Jody. I miss you so much. I want you so bad. I just want to hold you. Sometimes I squeeze my blanket, imagining it's you. Please say you'll be with me always. Tell me you love me, because it means so much. I love you and always will—no matter what.

I'm going to say some prayers now.

Jay

12

More Victims

It took four months and ten days for the Hillside Rapist to strike again after Sarah fought back. Psychologists describe this type of pause by serial rapists as a time when they obsess over unfulfilled fantasies. Often those obsessive thoughts build up until they explode into a new wave of attacks.

With his wounded hand and clawed-up face healed—and presumably with his ego nursed back into place, and his festering delusions of control at their full pathology—the Hillside Rapist struck again.

In October 1981, another attack was reported in the Cathedral Hill neighborhood. Life in the neighborhood had cautiously begun a fragile return to normalcy. People still had to go to work and return home. Children had to attend school. Cowering behind curtains and locked windows and doors was no way to live. This monster couldn't be allowed to win.

On October 9, in the broad daylight of midafternoon, a third victim, Mary, was brutally attacked and raped in a stairwell between a public walkway and a church while she was out for a run.

The vicious assault began a new crime spree so brazen the entire city went on full alert, the local media refocused their attention, and the frustrated Saint Paul police department intensified their efforts to get the Hillside Rapist off the streets and behind bars.

Mary

The Hillside Rapist no longer felt compelled to introduce himself as "Pat" or "Marty." The reporting officer used words like "brutal" and "forceful" to describe the attack on Mary, the third victim.

The officer's report noted that Mary was jogging up a public stairwell in the Cathedral Hill neighborhood. A man she described as "seventeen or eighteen years of age, wearing a blue baseball cap with white on the crown, a blue jean jacket and blue jeans with a brown belt" stopped her and asked for directions. She pointed toward the street he was looking for and continued on her way. He attacked her from behind, holding a "six-inch" knife to her throat and side, dragging her to nearby bushes. After the attack he said, "Don't fucking tell anyone." Then he fled on foot.

Over a harrowing five-month stretch—October 1981

through February 1982—the Saint Paul police department recorded ten more assaults, six resulting in rape. Another four victims reported being assaulted but decided against talking to the police or filing charges. They were too traumatized.

In total, the police would attribute sixteen assaults to the Hillside Rapist.

Thirty-two hours later he struck again.

Donna

Donna, a twenty-six-year-old vulnerable adult with a history of mental illness, was out for a walk. At the time she was living independently, trying to put her troubled life on track. She suffered from insomnia but had discovered that taking a walk before bedtime helped. It was just after midnight on October 11 when she stepped outside. She passed an alley where a man grabbed her and forced her back into the alley and behind a dumpster, where he assaulted her.

The first officers on the scene understood immediately that this was the work of the predator they were now calling the Hillside Rapist. The responding officers were male; the victim told them she would only talk to a female.

At the hospital, after the victim was treated, a female officer interviewed her and she opened up. She described her attacker: "white male, eighteen to twenty years old, five feet four, blond, curly hair spilling out from under a ball cap, jeans, blue jacket. He had a knife that he kept in a leather case." She said the rapist forced her to perform oral sex but did not "penetrate" her because "he couldn't get it up." She went on to describe him as "the craziest, most intense person I've ever seen. How can such a creepy little guy like that be so intense?"

The report of Donna's interview with the female police officer indicates she said, "I just feel so low. I can't trust my judgment. What did I do wrong? I must've done something really wrong for that to happen to me. How could I attract such a creepy little guy like that?"

The attending officer assured her she "did nothing wrong," that "a lot of victims feel that way after an assault." She explained it was "most likely a crime of circumstance." That Donna likely had just been in the wrong place at the wrong time. The female officer reflected that "none of this seemed to make her feel any better."

After a four-month break, the Hillside Rapist was back with a vengeance: two victims in two days. In less than a week he would attack again. The local media had latched onto the horrifying situation on Cathedral Hill. On Halloween, October 31, 1981, this short article appeared in the *Saint Paul Pioneer Press*:

3 HILL DISTRICT RAPES FOLLOW SAME PATTERN

Police are searching for a man they suspect of raping three women and attempting to rape a fourth recently in the Saint Paul Hill District.

The attacks occurred during a week's time.

"He generally attacks lone women, joggers, and strollers," the head of the Crimes Against Persons Unit said Tuesday. "It's usually late in the afternoon or at night."

The attacker usually uses a hunting knife that he carries in a sheath. In one case, when the man did not have the knife, the woman bit his hand and escaped.

The most distinguishing characteristic, however, is the cap the suspect wears. The victims have described it as a baseball cap, although the color and the bill size vary in their descriptions, indicating he may be wearing different caps.

In the first incident, a woman was raped after she was forced into some brush on the side of a stairwell. Two days later there was another attack in a nearby location. Two days after that, an attempted rape occurred in a nearby alley shortly after midnight.

The man is described as about seventeen or eighteen years old, five foot four to five foot six, with a medium build and blond, curly hair. Police said the man generally says very little during the attacks.

Samantha

During the next assault, the Hillside Rapist opened up to his victim in a brief, disturbing, and revealing conversation that sheds some light on the psyche of a serial rapist.

Samantha, a thirty-year-old woman, was going to work in the early morning hours of November 4, 1981. She worked the early shift at a Cathedral Hill business and always parked in what she thought was the safety of an underground parking lot. On the morning of the attack, she pulled in to her usual slot by the door, grabbed her purse, and began walking toward work "like I do every day," according to the police report. She only made it about twenty feet when a "white male, early twenties, five three, one hundred forty pounds, blond/brown hair parted in the middle and hanging out from under a blue cap, wearing a light-colored leather jacket, brown pants, and black boots" stepped out of a shadow and forced her back into her car.

She fought him. She kicked and punched and flailed and screamed. Eventually she stopped fighting because she just "wanted it to be over."

Samantha told her attacker, "I want you to stop. I am going to be late for work, and I don't want to be late for work. Stop."

That's when he opened up to her—during and after the rape. Here's how the police report documents it:

(During) "I don't want to stop. I'll stop when I want to stop."

(After) "Isn't it better when you just

cooperate?"

Victim made no reply.

"Was it good?"

Victim made no reply.

"I would like to see you again. Can I see you again?"

Victim made no reply.

"Under different circumstances. Can I see you again?"

Victim made no reply.

"Can I drive you to the front door?"

Victim shook her head no.

"I think you're an honest person. If I drive you to the door there wouldn't be anyone coming after me would there?"

Victim made no reply.

"You're not going to tell anyone, right?"

Victim shook her head no.

"I don't want you mad at me. I'm going to let you go because I don't want you mad at me."

Victim made no reply.

Suspect then suddenly bolted out of the vehicle but stopped once to yell back: "Don't be mad at me!"

Samantha entered her work building and did one thing before contacting security: she punched in. Her time card for that day read 4:16 a.m. She was sixteen minutes late for work, detained for twenty-one minutes of hell by the Hillside Rapist.

In a few bizarre, disturbing snippets of conversation with Samantha, the Hillside Rapist revealed an almost human side to the monster—a desire to connect, a pathetic need to have his victim not "be mad" at him, a futile, twisted attempt to make some kind of amends after his heinous crime: "Can I drive you to the front door?"

When the Hillside Rapist struck again two weeks later, no humanity was evident.

Marsha

November 18, 1981, was a beautiful autumn evening in Saint Paul, according to Marsha: "bright moon, cool and crisp but not yet freezing." The last leaves were falling and swirling down streets and alleys in a light breeze. The moon was well into the last phase of its cycle that night, almost fully visible.

Cloud cover and snow were expected later so Marsha, a fifty-one-year-old resident of the Cathedral Hill neighborhood, decided to take advantage of what could be the last nice evening for a long time; she went for a walk. Two blocks away from her apartment building she was accosted.

The police report details the attack:

A white male, seventeen to eighteen years old,
blondish, curly hair, five six, one hundred
forty to one hundred fifty pounds, full lips,
baby face, clean-shaven, reddish-maroon
waist-length jacket, light blue jeans, boots,
wearing a cap approached the victim and
asked directions . . . Before she answered, he
dragged her off the sidewalk behind a building
and at knifepoint demanded she remove her
pants. Victim stated, "I have a disease that,
trust me, you don't want to get. You better
not do this." The suspect questioned her but
eventually believed it to be true. The suspect
then stated, "You can [perform oral sex]."
Victim got angry and said, "I will not do that.
Make me do that, and I will bite it off." The
suspect then brandished the knife, put it to
her throat, turned her around, and penetrated
victim anally.

Before fleeing, the suspect demanded, "Don't look at
me." Snow had begun to fall by this time. Marsha made
her way back to her apartment and called the police.
Arrangements were made to transport the "badly shaken"
Marsha to St. Paul–Ramsey Medical Center. Employees of
the emergency room there were becoming accustomed by
this time to admitting rape victims from Cathedral Hill.

Tests were performed at the hospital on fluids obtained

from Marsha's body and clothing. The results of those tests would soon prove key to the case of alleged Hillside Rapist Jay Chapman. Marsha was the victim who, three months later, faced Jay Chapman in court.

The attacks were now coming fast and furious. A terrorized neighborhood was on full alert. A deeply frustrated police department was desperate to get the perpetrator off the streets.

Lisa

The assault on Lisa, the last recorded hillside rape of 1981, occurred on November 24 in a parking lot behind an apartment building. The victim had arrived home late from work. She was unlocking the door to her building when a man grabbed her from behind, put a knife to her throat, dragged her behind a van in the parking lot, and raped her. Suspect was described as a "white male, approximately five foot five, one hundred fifty pounds, wearing a cap, curly light brown hair, baby faced with a small, narrow mustache. He was wearing a rust-colored jacket and light-colored pants."

After providing the police with a description and being examined at the hospital, Lisa immediately left the city to be with her parents in northern Wisconsin. She was so traumatized it was weeks before she was ready to supply the police with further information. When she was strong enough to relive her attack, she spoke again to the police and shared the following statements.

"He was vicious. . . . I feared for my life. . . . He took his time to check his appearance afterwards. . . . He didn't seem worried about getting caught. . . . His breath was musty. Not smoky but musty . . . I hoped someone from my building had heard something and called the police."

When asked if she could identify her attacker, Lisa stated she was "dead certain" she could.

Lisa had a roommate at the time and attempts to contact him, and other residents of the building, were unsuccessful, as noted in the police report: "The victim shared an apartment with a male companion who did not accompany her to Wisconsin. He has never been contacted. Nor has he responded to requests (left on cards at the apartment) that he call the department. Other occupants of the building seem to be mostly Hmong and as such conversations are limited to grins, smiles, hand waving, and an occasional 'nyah Zhong!'—which has produced nothing but frustration."

(There is no Hmong phrase "nyah Zhong." It is, however, the general pronunciation of *nyob zoo*, which means "hello.")

Labeling the roommate a "companion" seems to have connotations not supported by any facts. It's also unclear how the officer knew the roommate didn't accompany Lisa to Wisconsin if he had never been contacted.

The description of the Hmong residents as a nonsensical group of grinning, hand-waving people reveals a clear lack of cultural sensitivity. It's also distressing that these residents were apparently never interviewed in the presence of an interpreter. A final note in the report regarding the victim makes the following conclusion, highlighting a police officer's lack of knowledge about the harrowing aftermath of a violent sexual assault: "One may surmise that she [the victim] has lost interest in the matter."

It's probably safer to surmise that Lisa will never be able to forget the matter. Common aftereffects of rape include depression, flashbacks, sleeping disorders, post-traumatic stress disorder, substance abuse, self-harm, and suicide. This is not an exhaustive list. Rape victims' after-effects can last a lifetime.

The residents of Cathedral Hill and many other Saint Paul residents definitely weren't losing interest in the case of the Hillside Rapist. The local media had glommed onto the story and were calling more and more attention to it. Intense pressure was being applied to the police to get this monster off the streets. All photographs in the Saint Paul police department of suspects who *might* fit the description of the rapist were being pulled and placed in a file labeled "highest priority."

In that file was a photo of Jay Chapman, who'd been taken in on a few occasions for minor infractions. At some point, a booking photo was taken.

Jay is five feet six, and at that time weighed approximately one hundred forty pounds. He wore his light brown hair on the longish side, so there was enough to spill out of a baseball cap. A peek at Jay's 1981–82 Central High year-book reveals nearly an entire class of young white males who wore their hair in pretty much the same way. It's probably not a coincidence that musicians in some of the most popular rock bands of the day—Van Halen, Journey, The Police, Foreigner—sport similar long-haired styles.

The police decided to narrow down their suspects based on the victims' descriptions. They also limited their scope to boys who had a police record and who lived in the neighborhood. Jay Chapman's photo made the cut.

13

According to Jody

During the months of October and November 1981, while the Hillside Rapist was on the second phase of his Summit Hill rampage, Jody Preimesberger was still chronicling the events of her life.

Jody appears to have loved her new habit of diary writing almost as much as she loved her new boyfriend. Her entries were now almost daily. The diary is a glimpse into the life of a happy high school senior going steady with a boy she loves, finishing school, working, and having a lot of fun. She's excited about what lies ahead after high school. She can't wait to move out and begin the adult portion of life with Jay, her one and only.

October 8, 1981

Went to school then went out with Jay. Just hung out, didn't do much of anything.

October 9, 1981

Went to school. Came home with Jay, and we just sat at my house. Then we drank some beer. I had a really good night because Jay slept over.

October 10, 1981

Jay had a party. I didn't drink that much, but Jay did. He got really drunk. We (Jay and I) ate at the St. Clair Broiler. Jay slept over and we had another good night.

October 11, 1981

Saturday, Jay was here during the day. That night Jay had another keg party at the valley. Bitched at Heather.

So according to Jody, on October 9, 1981, she went to school, came home with Jay, sat at her house all night drinking beer, and described it as a good night because Jay slept over. Mary, the third victim, was raped at 4 p.m. that afternoon, about the time Jody and Jay were getting home from school. She doesn't say whether Jay left for any period of time, just that they "sat at her house," eventually "drank beer," and that it was a good night because he "slept over." Could Jay have raped Mary? Possibly. Given the level of detail about Jay's activities and their time together Jody records in the diary, it doesn't seem as if Jody would've omitted that he left and returned. Nothing in her diary asserts they were together at exactly four o'clock—but it seems pretty clear that they were together the entire day, based on Jody's entry.

How about Donna, assaulted just over one day later at 12:25 a.m. on October 11? According to Jody, Jay hosted a beer drinking party the night of October 10 (spilling into the eleventh) at which he "got really drunk." Jay and Jody ate at the St. Clair Broiler at some point that evening, she doesn't say exactly when. After the party, Jody says they spent the night together. It was, she writes, "another good night," possibly a euphemism for having sex.

Is it possible that Jay found a way to extract himself from a party he was hosting, for at least an hour, go assault someone on Summit Hill, and then return to his own party without his absence being noted by his girlfriend?

Highly unlikely.

Also, Donna told police her attacker was very "intense," like he might be on drugs, but that she "did not smell alcohol on him." Jay was drinking that evening. All evening. So much so that Jody recorded, "Jay got really drunk." During the course of a lengthy, "intense" struggle, the victim would've almost certainly smelled alcohol on him.

Again, Mary's and Donna's descriptions of the attacker are nearly identical: five three or five four; one hundred to one hundred fifty pounds; light blond, light brown, or sandy hair; wearing a hat; brandishing a knife in a leather case. It's highly probable that the same person attacked both these women. It's almost impossible to deduce that Jay Chapman was that person because he was drunk as a lord at a keg party among many witnesses and most certainly smelled strongly of alcohol.

Jody's entries continue:

November 3, 1981

Went to school and got out at 10. Sat at Ramsey, then I played tennis, which I didn't play too hot. Then I went to Andy's for a bit. I got home at 9:20.

November 4, 1981

Went to school. Started working today, worked 1 to 3. After work went to Jay's house. We sat around. Then I helped Jay bring some stuff to Jeff's [Jay's brother] house. We went to Nagal's house. We drank. I got home around 7:30.

November 18, 1981

I worked from 11:30 to 2:15. I went over to Jay's and hung around for a while. Then we came back to my house and watched the tube, and then Jay went to BJ's. It's SNOWING!

November 24, 1981

No school. From 11:30 to 1:30, I sat around at Jay's house. Then we went over to BJ's.

Drank. Got home at 8. Made a payment of
$59.92.

Samantha, the fifth victim, was assaulted at 3:35 a.m.
on November 4 in a parking lot as she was arriving for
work. Her description of the assailant was very similar to
other descriptions of the Hillside Rapist during the second phase of his crime spree: five three, one hundred forty
pounds, skinny, and blond-brown hair.

Could Jay have committed this crime? Yes. He was
with Jody until 9:20 p.m. the previous evening. According to the diary, she didn't see him again until after three
o'clock the following afternoon, a seventeen-hour gap.
Samantha was raped during this time. Jay would have had
to slip out of his parents' house, commit the crime, and
return at close to five in the morning unnoticed by his
father, Jerry, who was an early riser. Tricky, but possible.

The rape of Marsha occurred on November 18 at 7:27
p.m. Her description of the assailant, again, is very similar
to previous statements: a white male, between seventeen
and eighteen years old, blondish, curly hair, five foot six,
one hundred forty to one hundred fifty pounds, full lips,
"baby face," clean-shaven, reddish-maroon waist-length
jacket, light blue jeans, and boots.

Jody was with Jay until arriving home at eight that
evening. Could Jay have committed this rape? Unlikely,
unless Jody's timeline was off by an hour. But her diary is
quite precise with exact times and dates. Jay would have
had to leave Jody's company and travel nearly three miles
and back to rape Marsha—all in the hour before Jody

records parting company with him.

Lisa, the seventh victim attributed to the Hillside Rapist, was assaulted on November 24. According to Jody she was with Jay all that day. She says she "sat around" at Jay's from 11:30 to 1:30 because there was "no school" on this day. She later states that "we went over to BJ's" and returned home at eight. She records she paid "$59.92" for something; it's not clear what the payment was for, but it illustrates the type of precise detail Jody was in the habit of recording.

Could Jay have committed this crime? No. He was with Jody during the commission of this crime. It happened between seven and eight in the evening, when he was with Jody. You'd have to wholesale reject this alibi to suspect Jay of this crime. At the very least, Jody should've been questioned about her entries. Her testimony could have corroborated Jay's assertion of innocence, and it might have helped the police locate other witnesses who could report Jay's presence somewhere other than the crime scenes.

Lisa's description of her attacker was similar to the previous accounts: "five foot four, one hundred fifty pounds, wearing a cap, curly light-brown hair, baby face with a small, narrow mustache. The suspect was wearing a rust-colored jacket and light-colored pants."

A review of the Hillside Rapist's reign of terror during the months of October and November 1981 reveals five assaults almost certainly perpetrated by the same man, based on the similar physical descriptions given by the victims, the use and description of a knife, and the brazen mode of the stalk and attack.

Jay Chapman was unaccounted for and couldn't be ruled out for the assaults on October 9 and November 4. On November 18 and November 24, it was physically possible but highly improbable Jay was anywhere near the scenes of the attacks. On October 11, there is no way Jay could have committed this crime.

Remarkably, Jody bought her diary just as she was beginning her relationship with Jay. Her passion for journaling grew alongside her love for Jay. And her journals provide a lot of information germane to Jay Chapman's activities during the time he was accused of being the Hillside Rapist. Jody's diary contains a passage for nearly every day of 1981 (a practice she would continue for many years to follow). She consistently marked the beginning and end times of the events of her life, almost all of which involved Jay Chapman. Jody and Jay were inseparable in their first year of dating, spending nearly every available moment together.

It's difficult to fathom why none of the Saint Paul police department investigators assigned to the Hillside Rapist case chose to follow up with Jody in any way after her diary was made available to them. Perhaps they believed she fabricated or doctored a diary to defend her boyfriend. Or they thought it wouldn't hold up in court.

Jody used many different pens with various ink colors as she wrote in her diary. The handwriting shows subtle changes throughout. Some passages appear to have been scribbled when she was pressed for time. Others flow in a beautiful, studied cursive replete with hearts to dot the i's and cheerful smiley faces to add emphasis. The entries become more frequent—and more verbose—as her comfort with journaling grew. It seems improbable, from a careful analysis of the content and the patterns of the entries, that she went back and re-created a diary after the fact.

Even setting all that aside, it just doesn't really make sense. If Jody had decided to make an elaborate fake diary, wouldn't she have crafted alibis for each assault rather than just some of them? Her entries don't account for Jay's whereabouts during several of the attacks.

By November, the Hillside Rapist was done for 1981, at least as far as official police records are concerned. Other assaults may have gone unreported before, during, or after the seven so far attributed to the same perpetrator.

The holiday season came and went in 1981 without a reported assault. Just after the New Year, that would change.

Crime spree number three was about to begin, and Jay Chapman's photo continued to make the cut as investigators winnowed suspects, frantically trying to figure out who was committing these crimes so they could make an arrest. A terrorized and outraged community was growing more and more vocal and the Saint Paul police department was feeling the heat.

Letter from Jail
Day 22

Jody,

I have a headache from crying on the telephone. It was so good to talk to you. My body feels weak and I am very pale. I need a workout—like fucking you all night long. That sounds great. I know you can't wait either cuz you told me that. I get excited thinking about it. My heart starts pumping faster. I better stop now, it's time to go eat. More after supper, my love.

Jody,

I just locked my door for the night. I am so tired. I want to be alone so I can think about the most beautiful thing in the world, and that's you. I love you so much. I am so lonely. I've been in here too long. I don't deserve this treatment. I pray that judge lets me out of here. I feel like crying all the time. I hang on by thinking about you. I'm going to try to sleep. I'll finish this in the morning.

Jay loves Jody so much.

Good morning, Jody,

I just got out of the shower and my hair is dripping wet. Right now I'm having a cig and combing my hair and wishing I were with you. Today at 11 a.m. I'm talking to my lawyer, the public defender. I have a feeling tomorrow is the big day to find out what's going to happen. I hope it's for the good. That test should be coming back, and I know the results will be negative and this nightmare will be over.

If the test isn't negative for some reason, I guess I'm up shit creek. I have a book called *Good News for Modern Man*, and I'm going to read some of it later. I need some good news.

All I know for sure is that as long as you're on my side, I'm going to get through this.

Jay

14

Still More Victims

Kristin

On the evening of January 25, 1982, shortly after eleven o'clock, the Hillside Rapist struck again. A nineteen-year-old college student had been studying late at school. When she hopped a bus home, a man in the rear of the bus moved up to sit next to her. She moved to a different seat. He followed.

The victim got off the bus in the Cathedral Hill neighborhood. So did the man. The victim began to run. The assailant caught her and forced her off the sidewalk. They struggled until the man pointed a knife at her and demanded she remove her clothes. She kicked the knife out of his hand. As the rapist moved to retrieve it, she ran again.

He chased her, tackled her, and was ripping at her pants just as a car was turning the corner. The car's headlights washed over the assailant holding a knife to Kristin's throat. She screamed. The rapist panicked and ran away. Kristin made it to her apartment, where she called her mother and then the police. Her description of the man was one the Saint Paul police had heard before: "approximately eighteen years old, five foot five, one hundred fifty pounds, sandy hair, smooth face, wearing a cap and a rust-colored jacket with blue coloring on the shoulders."

The police showed her an array of pictures that included the booking shot of Jay Chapman, who was now their main suspect. Kristin looked at the photo of Jay and said, "the eyes might be familiar but nothing else."

While Kristin managed to get away before being raped, the Hillside Rapist's next victim wasn't so lucky.

Jackie

On Friday, January 29, at around eight o'clock in the evening, a twenty-six-year-old woman was standing on a corner waiting for a girlfriend. They planned to walk to a restaurant together for dinner. A man appeared and asked her if she knew where "the old folks' home" was located. She told him no and walked away. He followed her, and then grabbed her. "We're gonna go fuck," he said. He shoved her behind a tree and, at knifepoint, ordered her to remove the overalls she was wearing. She told him that under her overalls she was wearing full body-length underwear that was "really hard to take off." He put the knife to her throat and ordered her to perform oral sex. Afterward, she told police, he "walked away like he wasn't worried at all about getting caught." Jackie made her way back to the corner and found her girlfriend, who called the police for her.

She declined to go to the hospital. She described her assailant as "slim, five foot five to five foot seven, one hundred thirty pounds, wearing a stocking cap, a jacket, blue jeans, and boots." She stated the knife looked like a "big steak knife." She described the rapist's voice as "a little raspy."

Amy

Two days later, on Sunday, January 31, a thirty-eight-year-old woman exited her car in the Cathedral Hill neighborhood around 8:15 p.m. She approached her apartment building carrying shopping bags. A man seemed to "step out of nowhere" and asked her for directions to a nearby street. The woman pointed the way. The man pulled out a knife and said, "You're coming with me."

They walked into a nearby alley, where the man shoved her farther down the alley. "Get rid of your packages," he said. "Take off your pants." Amy asked him if he was going to kill her, and he replied, "Not if you do what I say." She indicated that if the man put down the knife, she'd do as he said. He hid the knife up his sleeve, and

Amy ran down the alley. The man caught her, pushed her down and attempted to kiss her. The woman fought him. "I am not going to let you do this to me," she told him. Just then a truck turned into the alley and startled them. The man got up and said, "See ya later."

The woman made her way back to her apartment and called the police.

Amy provided another familiar description: "white male, seventeen years old, five foot six, one hundred forty pounds, wavy, light-brown hair over the collar, small amount of acne on face, thin nose, wearing a dark-colored parka w/o hood (quilted), blue jeans, dark gloves and a hat." The knife was described as a five-inch steak knife with a brown plastic handle.

The media was on full alert. The outraged Twin Cities community was demanding action. All three local TV network affiliates had aired stories about a "monster" loose on the streets. At least three articles appeared in the Saint Paul newspaper featuring the Hillside rapes.

On August 22, 1982, the *Saint Paul Pioneer Press* published a story quoting a number of local women who were angry and frustrated that the attacks kept happening. One told the reporter, "This has altered the way I see all men." Others said the crimes had altered their everyday behaviors. "I have become very rude," one said. Another explained, "I don't get on an elevator alone with a man anymore."

One woman was quoted as saying, "I am frustrated and disgusted by a police department that does not give us enough information or protection; by politicians who don't care; by media that don't give enough coverage to these rapes; by a legal system that seems to require the capture of a rapist in the act before you can get a prosecution." Another woman said, "The emotional damage is irreparable." It's likely they all would have agreed with the woman who summed it all up: "There is no such thing as going back to the way things were."

The assault on Amy on January 31, 1982, was the last recorded crime of the Hillside Rapist. The police had a suspect who fit the description, was known to them, and who lived near the area. They had an outraged community demanding an arrest. Their next move was to round up their main suspect: Jay Chapman.

Jody Preimesberger's first diary, which has a final entry from New Year's Day 1982, has no further insight into the accusation that Jay was the Hillside Rapist; she ran out of pages. Her final entries of 1981 sum up her life succinctly and clearly, just before it became clouded by doubt, shame, frustration, and anger thanks to the allegations aimed at her boyfriend.

December 30, 1981

This has been the best year of my life. Went snowmobiling for a bit today, sat around, then went home at four. Had a few troubles with the car. Jay got frustrated. Went to a party and got drunk. Got into an argument with Jay, and he kind of slapped me a couple times.

I suppose I can forgive him because of my love for him . . .

Late with my pill.

December 31, 1981

Had a long talk with Jay. He said he was sorry (for hitting me). He said he could not live without me. This made me so happy I could have cried. He said it would never happen again. We stayed at the duplex his dad owned which we sometimes do when it isn't occupied. We had a wonderful time alone together in bed. He is the one and only person I will always love. I love my Jay. He is my baby.

January 1, 1982

Worked, 11 to 2. Sat around at the duplex. Threw some snowballs at the store. Stayed at the duplex and had a good time with my baby in bed. I am very happy today.

Jody didn't get a new diary until mid-February 1982. Her very first entry in her brand-new diary sets the tone for the next phase of her life.

February 18, 1982

Jay is arrested.

15

Outrageous Violators

According to the fifth edition of the *Diagnostic and Statistical Manual of Mental Disorders* (DSM-5), the authoritative resource for clinicians and physicians to diagnose psychiatric illnesses, "rape is a crime, not a mental disorder."

But according to a 2018 study published by the medical journal *The Lancet Child & Adolescent Health*, 80 percent of teenage girls who have been raped will suffer a serious mental illness as a result of the crime.

The 1979 book *Men Who Rape: The Psychology of the Offender* by clinical psychologist A. Nicholas Groth is still considered one of the best resources for understanding the psyche of a rapist. Groth categorizes rapists into four groups:

- *anger rapists*, who are driven by antisocial aggression that's usually prevalent from a very early age

- *power rapists*, who crave power and control to address feelings of inadequacy about their masculinity and sexual ability

- *sadistic rapists*, who want to degrade and humiliate their victims as a more extreme way of feeling powerful and in control

- *opportunistic rapists*, whose offenses are unplanned and impulsive

Opportunistic rapists are seeking immediate sexual gratification, and they use force as necessary. Opportunistic rapists are often known to the victim, and their crimes are often driven by circumstances rather than psychopathology. For example, late at night, lone isolated female, no witnesses around, and so on.

The Hillside Rapist was definitely an opportunistic rapist, randomly preying on lone women often moments after they appeared on the street. But he also exhibited anger, sadism, and vindictiveness—along with a preoccupation of sexual fantasies and urges ("Was I good?" he asked Ellen), and a desire to degrade and humiliate the victims. Like all rapists, he was driven by a sick need to wield power and control.

The Saint Paul police were hunting a sexual predator—and he seemed to be getting bolder. And he was young—seventeen to twenty-four years old. Surely it must have been frightening to imagine what this early behavior would become over time.

His growing boldness and vindictiveness were evident during the third phase of his crime spree. The attacks were now often in the open, followed by the rapist cavalierly walking away rather than running.

The case of the Hillside Rapist had become a top priority in the department.

16

Second Arrest

My father received a phone call from the attorney two weeks after my juvenile detention. He had a shocking update: the police were going to put out a warrant for my arrest. I should go turn myself in before that happened, he said. So the next day my dad drove me downtown to turn myself in.

"Stay strong," he told me, "this will all be over soon."

I walked up the stairs to the police station. They seemed really wide and steep for such a small building. I felt like I was walking up the stairs to the Minnesota state capitol. I opened the building's huge doors. They were heavy.

I approached the glass window, behind which was a man in uniform. He said, "May I help you?" I stared at his badge. I was struck by how clean it was, how the light in the room bounced off it. It was blinding. I thought he must shine that badge every day. I bet he spit shines it.

In as even a voice as I could muster, I said, "My name is Jay Perry Chapman, and I'm here to turn myself in."

The officer looked at me a moment. "Have seat over there." He made a call and kept an eye on me.

Soon an elevator door opened, and there stood another man in uniform. His badge was also very shiny. I could see my reflection in it. "Please step into the elevator, Mr. Chapman," he said. "We're going upstairs for your booking." My knees weakened a bit as I stepped in the elevator. My armpits started to drip. I really didn't know what was going to happen next.

We got off on the second floor, where I was led to a holding cell. Four other guys were there to be processed. We entered and the door closed behind me with a bang.

My escort handed someone behind a desk a slip of paper and said, "This is Chapman, Jay. He's here on a first-degree charge." I didn't know exactly what that meant, but I didn't like the sound of it.

I started talking to the other men in the holding cell. One guy said he was there on his second DWI. Another said he was up on a domestic-abuse charge. The other two claimed they were in a bar fight. One had a black eye, the other a split lip. I never found out if they were fighting each other or not.

All of a sudden I heard another voice from down the hallway, screaming, like he was in agony: "Let me outta here! Please, let me outta here!"

The officers just ignored him. He kept it up for at least

five minutes: "Get me outta here! I gotta get outta here!"

Finally an officer went over to him and said, "Shut up or you're going to the hole." He didn't shut up, so they took him away. I could hear him screaming down a hallway for a long time. Then it was quiet again.

After about thirty minutes a door opened and an officer stepped through it. "Chapman," he said, "this way."

I was told to put all my belongings on a counter.

"Turn to the wall and put your hands up."

I did.

"Put your feet there."

I did, on two footprints in the floor.

"Take off your socks." He turned my socks inside out to see if I had something inside. Then he frisked me—checked under my armpits, ran his hands down my body, felt in my pockets, then ran his hands up and down my legs. "Put your socks back on."

He grabbed a miniature paint roller and a bottle of ink. He passed the roller over a flat surface. He told me to give him my left hand first and pressed each finger, one by one, into the inked surface and then onto a paper. My thumb was last. He took my right hand and did the same thing. He sprayed my hands with fluid. "Rub," he said. Then he handed me a paper towel. "This way."

He opened a door and suddenly we were in a hallway of cells. The adult jail felt very different than the juvenile detention center where I'd been before. It was darker, more ominous. We passed cell after cell after cell. We must've passed twenty of them, all full of prisoners. I could feel their stares, but I didn't want to make eye contact.

To my right was a row of windows. I looked out one and across Interstate 94 I could see the Taystee Bakery where they baked bread and pastries. I was put into a cell on the Taystee side of the aisle. The other side was dark. I learned that's where they put guys who didn't listen so well.

This must be what it feels like to be a dog in a kennel, I thought. That cell was my home for the next four days. I didn't sleep that first night. I had so much on my mind. I was wondering what Jody was doing. Each hour seemed like a day.

Early the next morning, they handed out a donut, an orange, and a carton of milk for breakfast. I gobbled it up, I was so hungry. A couple of hours went by and I was brought up front for my mug shots. I'd been talking to my next-cell neighbor the night before. He was in for DWI. It was weird not knowing what he looked like, so when they let me out for my mug shot, I said hello and we fist-bumped.

I continued down the hallway and entered the mug shot room. The lady said, "Look forward." She snapped a shot. "Turn to the side!" She snapped another shot. Then an officer brought me back to my cell.

I guess that was my excitement for the day. I remember staring out across the freeway at the Taystee Bakery sign. *I'll never eat that bread again for as long as I live.*

The day dragged on. Lunch came, and I ate everything. They barely give you enough food to survive. I asked the guard if I could use the phone. "No," he said. "You'll have to wait your turn." The afternoon crept by and then it was dinnertime—still no phone.

Dinner was served. The portions of food they give you would barely fill up a ten-year-old kid. After dinner I asked the guard again if I could use the phone. "It's coming down the line," he said. "Wait your turn." I guess I was the end of the line because it seemed to take forever. Finally the guard asked who I wanted to call. I said my parents. I gave him the number. He dialed and handed me the receiver. My father answered and as soon as I heard his voice I started to cry. It just hit me, how miserable and lonely I was in that place. He said there is no bail set for me yet and I have to stay until they set bail. Apparently the police were building their case against me.

I asked Dad if he'd talked with Jody. He said he had, and she's very concerned about what's going on. I wanted to talk to her so badly. I kept crying. I considered myself a tough guy, but this was really awful. I couldn't help myself. We talked for a few more minutes until the guard said, "Chapman!" I told my dad I love him, and he said the same thing back to me.

I handed the phone back to the guard and asked when I would get another phone call. He said the next morning.

Back in my cell, I laid down and stared at the ceiling, scanning my cell. I rolled over and looked at all the graffiti on the walls, guys' names scratched into the paint. I looked at the stainless-steel toilet, pissed in by God knows how many people before I got here. I suddenly jumped off the bunk and scrubbed it with soap and toilet paper. I did a pretty good job scrubbing that toilet. I jumped back up on the top bunk and stared at those walls again. The night rolled by like molasses. It was very hard to fall asleep in that place, but I finally did.

I woke the next day to the door banging and clanging. Breakfast time. Another donut and an orange. I asked for my morning phone call. "It's coming down the line," I was told. More waiting.

Just before lunch an investigator came to my cell with a guard. "Chapman, we want to talk with you." They brought me down the long hall again, past all the cells. We arrived at a room where they sat me down and started drilling me with more questions.

"Do you ever hang out by Cathedral Hill or even drive by there?"

I said not really.

"Do you know where Boyd Park is?"

I said no.

"Do you ever drive down Western Avenue at all?"

I said no.

"Never?"

"That's just not a street I'm usually on."

I could tell the investigator was getting mad. He asked a bunch more questions and I just kept saying no, never been there, don't know where that is. I was telling the truth. They eventually brought me back to my cell. I jumped up on the top bunk and the guy in the cell next to me asked what happened. "Nothing," I told him. "Talked to an investigator. He asked me a bunch of questions. I tried to answer them. He got pissed off."

My neighbor said, "Fuck him."

After lunch the phone finally got to me and I called Jody. I was so happy to hear her voice, to talk to her. She told me how much she loved me and I told her I loved her. I began to cry again. Something about hearing the voices of people I loved on the outside was more than I could bear, I guess. The thought of not being able to see them again tapped into a deep sorrow. Jody tried to assure me everything would be all right. She said she talked to my lawyer. She told him she had a diary she'd been writing in almost every day, and she gave it to him. She told the lawyer she thought it might help. I'm sure this felt like a violation to her, there was an awful lot of private stuff in her diary. That told me how much she loved me. We talked as long as the guard let us—seemed like just a few minutes. I told her I couldn't wait to put my arms around her again. Eventually there was the guard again: "Chapman! You're done."

They took me back to my cell. I hopped up on my bunk and just lay there, reliving every word Jody and I had spoken and wondering when this nightmare would be over.

The next afternoon, a guard came wandering down the hall waving a pack of Marlboro Red cigarettes. That just happens to be the brand I smoke. I didn't realize it at the time, but I was being targeted.

When he got right in front of my cell the guard held those cigarettes up and announced, "I need a volunteer! Does anyone want to go be in a lineup? There's a pack of cigarettes in it for you!"

My hand shot up.

I'd been in that cell for three days doing nothing—with no cigarettes. I would've done just about anything for those Marlboro Reds.

He gave me the cigarettes. "All right, Chapman. Here you go." Then he opened my cell. "C'mon."

He pointed me down the hall. "Walk." He followed very closely behind as we passed other cells. *Out of all these guys, he picked me.* I felt kind of special, like—*what did I do to win these cigarettes? My brand!* I was a little naïve back then.

I was led into a room where four other guys were already waiting. We didn't really make eye contact, so I didn't get a good look at them at first. We were told to walk in front of a white background. Really bright lights burned down on us. I couldn't see anything in front of me.

A voice said, "Just stand there and look forward!"

I suddenly felt self-conscious about my appearance. I must look a wreck. I had long hair at that time, I hadn't washed it in three days. I hadn't showered in four days. I didn't even have a comb in jail.

As I stared forward I realized, *The guy who did this horrible crime is probably standing in this lineup with me.*

"Turn to the right!"

We all did.

"Turn to the left!"

While we were turning, I finally got a good look at the other guys in the lineup. None of them looked anything like me. At the time, that made me feel safe. *Surely the victim will be able to pick out the right one. We all look really different from each other.*

When it was over, they put us all on the same elevator with guards to go back upstairs. I peeked around at those other guys. *It's because of one of you that I'm in this horrible place.* I'm pretty sure one of the guys in the lineup was a police investigator.

They brought me back to the cell, and I crawled onto the top bunk. It's where I liked to hang out, as far away from everyone as I could get. Not long after that, my lawyer was let into my cell. He asked how I was doing. "I'm very bored," I told him. "When are you going to get me out of here?"

Then he hit me with some news. "Jay, you need to know the whole story. Sixteen women have been assaulted in the Cathedral Hill neighborhood in the past year—all within about a mile radius of each other. Ten of them were raped at knifepoint. They all gave a description of a guy who looks about like you. The police believe they're looking for one assailant, a serial rapist. And they think you're him. At the lineup you just volunteered to be a part of— five of those women were standing behind the glass. The investigator just told me all five stated with 99 percent certainty that you were the man who raped them."

"Oh my God. You've got to be kidding me."

"They have until tomorrow to charge you or let you

go." He told me Jody had given him his diary. He'd looked through it, and he believed it would help. He planned to use it in my defense.

"What now?"

"Don't talk to anybody about this. Don't volunteer for any more lineups. I hope to get you out of here tomorrow on bail."

Oh my God—how are my parents going to come up with more bail money?

The lawyer called for a guard, and they escorted him out. As he left, the situation began settling in.

This was some serious shit.

After lunch an investigator came to my cell. In his hands were knives and ball caps I recognized as my own. The investigator started holding up knives.

"These are the knives you used on those women, Chapman. We know that now."

"That's my knife, but I don't know what you're talking about."

"You were just picked out by five victims. Every one of them stated you're the guy. Just tell me about using these knives on those women and this will go a lot easier for you."

They weren't asking me anymore, they were telling me I did it.

"I don't know what you're talking about."

Then he got very angry. His face turned red. He raised his voice and he started shoving knives in my face. "Tell me what you know about these knives. Right fucking now!" I thought he was going to hit me.

I wanted to say, *Fuck you, you bastard. You don't know what you're talking about.* Instead I took my lawyer's advice, I shut up and said nothing. I found out later the police procured search warrants, tore through my car, and searched my parents' house from top to bottom. They turned my room inside out, my parents' room, our whole house. They even took knives out of the kitchen drawer. I couldn't imagine how my parents felt, especially my mom.

The investigator finally left, and I lay back on my bunk. *What a prick. What a nightmare.* I kept telling myself that this would pass, that it had to. But I was starting to feel really frightened. I'd always heard innocent people don't go to prison. *Yes, sometimes they do . . .*

Later that night I finally got to make a phone call. It seemed like it took forever to get down the line to me. "Dad, they're trying to convict me of a terrible crime. They're saying I'm the guy who raped all these women."

"I know. Try not to worry. Your lawyer feels pretty sure we can get you out of there in the morning. They have a DNA sample of the rapist. We're going to get this cleared up."

We chatted for what seemed like just a few more seconds before a guard walked up. "Chapman! One minute."

I wanted to say, *Fuck you, asshole. I've been waiting for hours to use the phone, and I've only been on for a minute.* But I didn't. You piss those guys off, and they can make life hell for you. "Yes, sir."

Dad and I finished up, and I handed the guard the

phone. "Thank you, sir."

I was escorted back to my cell.

An hour later the guard returned to my cell and offered me a shower. First shower I'd been offered in four days. I couldn't wait for a shower, but I said, "No, thank you. I'm getting out in the morning. I'll shower at home."

"Suit yourself."

Luckily that's what happened. The next morning they came to my cell and said, "Let's go, Chapman."

We walked down the long hallway and stopped at the counter, where they returned my property: twenty bucks and half a pack of Marlboro Reds.

Then we got on the elevator, and the guard hit the button for the first floor. Down we went—and out I went onto the street. *Oh my God, I'm out of there—after four days.* I went straight home and straight into the shower. I never felt so dirty in my life. Four days in a goddam jail cell will do that to you. I scoured my body twice. Then I called Jody.

She was waiting for my call. "Get over here!"

She didn't need to ask twice. I couldn't wait to see her, put my arms around her again, and tell her how much I loved her. And thank her for offering up her diary. I knew what a big deal that was for her, and what an act of love it was. My hair was still wet when I got there. I gave her a big kiss. "C'mon."

"Where we going?"

"I have an appointment at the hospital for a DNA test. But I want you with me—from now on."

17

Certainty

The police report that describes the lineup Jay volunteered to be in reflects a different story than Jay heard from the investigator and his lawyer.

Five men were in the lineup. Jay was number three. According to the report written immediately after the lineup, only number four in the group was never mentioned as a possible suspect. The five victims who viewed the lineup pointed to suspects one, two, three, and five as possibly being their attacker. Two victims said numbers one and three "have a strong resemblance" to their attacker. Another claimed number two was "the most familiar looking." At the time of the lineup, none of the victims who participated could say with certainty that they were looking at their attacker—let alone with "99 percent certainty," as Jay's lawyer was told by an investigator.

Jerry Chapman paid Jay's bail with more borrowed

money, and the police were forced to let Jay go while they continued to attempt to bolster a case against him. They were no longer seeking anyone else for the series of Hillside rapes. As far as the police were concerned, Jay Chapman was their guy.

18

Lie Detector

I wanted Jody with me all the time now. And that's where she wanted to be. It was hard going back to school. Word had leaked out about me being arrested, and I knew everyone, the other kids and the staff, was talking about me. I could face it as long as I had Jody. I asked Jody to switch out of the regular school program she was in and join me in School Within School. Jody was very intelligent and didn't need to be in that program, but she said she would.

My SWS teacher's name was Johnny Bland. He couldn't believe what was happening to me outside of school. Mr. Bland was a black man in his late forties. He was very wise, and he really cared about his students. He helped get Jody into SWS with me so we could be together. He told me a police investigator had actually called him to ask what he thought of me.

"What did you tell him?"

He smiled. "I told him the truth."

I asked what that meant.

"I told them you spend most of your time with your girlfriend, who seems like a very nice girl. I told them you always, eventually, finish the work I give you to do. I told them you're a C+ student and that when you're not here or with your girlfriend, you're working with your dad. And as far as I know—that's the truth."

I was grateful for Mr. Bland. I could tell he believed in me and wanted to help. That meant the world to me. He was kind and supportive when I most needed it. I'll never forget that.

Word of my arrest spread fast. Not everyone I knew was as steadfast as my mom, Jody, and Mr. Bland in their belief that I was innocent. Some friends and neighbors offered their support, but the phone calls and visits slowly dried up. My whole family became a little isolated during that time. It sounds cliché, but it's true: when stuff like this happens you truly find out who your real friends are.

My mom remembered that part of the experience like this:

> It immediately affected my son and our
> entire family. It was decided that he could
> finish high school, but after a while it became
> obvious he would have a hard time finishing
> on campus. He finished high school at home

so he wouldn't have to go through the trauma of facing other students, many of whom had made up their mind about Jay. My daughter's friends were no longer able to sleep overnight in our home. Before the arrest there was always someone spending the night. The stigma of my son being the Hillside Rapist left parents ill at ease. They made excuses for why they were canceling, but it became obvious after a while. Can you blame them for protecting their daughters? I can't, but still I'm bitter. So is my husband.

My youngest son, five at the time, remembers Jay's second arrest, the house being surrounded by police cars and having the police traipse through our home, searching every room, including the kitchen. He was traumatized by it. Deeply traumatized. It instilled in him a frightening image of the police as intruders. No one in our family has a very positive image of the police anymore, not after this harrowing experience. We felt like prisoners, like the whole world had already found us guilty and passed judgment. I was no longer able to leave the house to take my baby boy to preschool. It dawned on me that an accusation like the one leveled at Jay rendered not just him but our entire family victims.

My mom was pretty smart. She put two and two together and realized there was no way I could've committed those crimes. She used to go over and over it. When I left the house to escort Jody home, it was almost always on foot, and I was never gone for more than an hour. To rape women on Cathedral Hill I'd have to take a bus down Grand Avenue and back, a five-mile round trip, or walk there really fast, find a victim, attack and rape with a knife, then walk back home by ten o'clock. My mom did the math and figured out it would take someone at least three hours to accomplish that task.

I wasn't exactly comfortable having my mom try to figure out how long it would take me to go rape someone, but after a while I got used to it.

Then my lawyer had an idea. "Let's take a lie detector test." I agreed, not knowing anything about how polygraph tests worked and not knowing that they were inadmissible in court anyway. Anything to get me out of this jam. I would do whatever it took to prove my innocence. Maybe this would do the trick.

The day of the lie detector test arrived. My dad told me to comb my hair, dress in my nice clothes, and look professional. So that's what I did. I drove to an address in Falcon Heights, a suburb of Saint Paul, in my dad's truck, which he almost never allowed me to drive other than to put into the garage. I was surprised to arrive at a residence, not an office. I walked up to the front door of this house and rang the bell. A man answered the door and asked me my name. He said it would take a minute to set up the test, so I should have a seat.

I was left alone in the living room of this strange house and almost immediately felt like I was being watched. I'm not usually paranoid like that, but I couldn't shake the feeling that someone was watching me—that I was under surveillance. I actually got up and peeked around the office, looking for a hidden camera. I think the strain of everything was starting to finally really wear on me.

When the man finally returned my anxiety was high. I could feel sweat running down my arms. The man said, "Follow me." He led me into a different room, sat me down next to a scary-looking machine, and began quietly affixing wires to my body. No words were exchanged. I got more nervous as each wire was affixed. The tester finally said, "Try to relax. I'm going to now ask you a series of questions."

I remember how scared I was of the machine. I didn't know how it worked, and being mechanically inclined, I like to know how things work. It looked like a machine that could be used to electrocute someone. My thoughts were racing. I definitely wasn't relaxed. I kept thinking, *Please God, don't let me die right now.*

The questioning began:

"Ever ride on a city bus?"

"Yes."

"Ever been to the park on Selby and Western?"

"I don't think so."

"Yes or no!"

"No."

"Ever been inside the Cathedral of Saint Paul?"

"Yes."

"Ever been to the James J. Hill House?"

"Yes."

The tester asked about twenty questions like this, pretty innocent questions until, out of the blue, the big one.

"Ever raped anyone?"

I felt my heart start to beat so hard I was sure the tester could hear it. My breath was suddenly very short.

"No."

I remember the whirring of the machine, moving rods and rustling paper. The sweat, running down my arms was now bleeding all the way through my nice clothes. I remember almost nothing that was asked by the tester for the remainder of my time wired to that machine, except that it mostly had to do with assaults and rapes and knives.

I was relieved when the tester suddenly announced, "That's it. We're done."

I left as quickly as I could. That night my father asked how I thought the test went and I told him, "Fine, I guess." I had nothing to compare it to, it was the strangest thing I'd ever done. The next day I found out how I really did when my lawyer called to tell us the results. "You failed."

"What?" I couldn't believe it—this just kept getting worse.

"You failed the test, but don't worry," he said. "They're very unreliable, those tests. And even if you passed, I probably couldn't have used it in court anyway. They're usually inadmissible."

Then why did I take it? I've never felt so uncomfortable as when I took that polygraph test. I don't know how anyone can get wired up like that and not feel guilty while taking one. Also, it was another apparently pointless expense for my parents.

Today the average cost to administer a lie detector test in the United States is between two hundred and two thousand dollars. It's a two-billion-dollar industry. In 1982, when Jay took the test, it cost between five and nine hundred dollars.

The polygraph test had a very shaky reputation up until 1984, when Ronald Reagan issued National Security Decision Directive 84, which regulated the test. The measure called for stricter scientific study and better methodologies in response to the polygraph's growing reputation for being widely unreliable.

Polygraphs assess physiological responses while a subject is asked and answers a series of questions. Among the responses measured are blood pressure, pulse, respiration, and skin conductivity. The theory is that deceptive answers will cause physiological responses that are measurably different than truthful answers. However, unlike Pinocchio's expanding nose, lying doesn't produce specific, reliable physiological reactions.

Eighteen-year-old Jay was traumatized by having to take a lie detector test that, according to the administrator, he "failed." Now there was more doubt, more anxiety, and more fear. Then the bill for the lie detector test arrived: five hundred dollars. Jerry Chapman paid it. More debt.

19

Death in the Family

Excruciating days went by. Then the phone rang late one night. Dad answered. It was my grandmother, Irene, calling from the West Coast. She was crying. She said my grandfather, Dan Chapman, had just died. They were in Las Vegas. They would rent an apartment in Las Vegas for five months out of the year to escape the Midwest winters.

My grandma reported that she'd gone out that evening to a casino. When she came back to the apartment, my grandfather was lying in the bedroom on the bed. Dead. He must have passed in his sleep. She said it appeared that "the Lord took his life in a very peaceful way. He looked very serene." No suffering. That's the way I want to go when it's my time.

When Dad told us kids what happened we all cried. My grandfather was a very loving, giving, and understanding guy. We were devastated by his sudden death.

Dad got on the phone with my grandmother and told her he'd be on the first flight he could catch out of Saint Paul. An hour later he was out the door with just a carry-on bag. He wanted to be by his mother's side as fast as he could, and he didn't want to wait for his luggage in Las Vegas. I'm sure he was the first guy off that plane. Dad helped her make the arrangements to have the body flown back to Saint Paul for a proper funeral. I just couldn't believe the pain, agony, and stress my dad must have been going through at that time. His son was getting accused of rape, and his father passed away.

At the funeral we met up with lots of family friends. The ones who were closest to us asked how my father and I were handling the rape case. We told them we were dealing with it the best way we knew how. One day at a time. This was terrifying new territory for us.

After the funeral we drove to Fort Snelling National Cemetery to bury my grandfather. An honor guard was there to pay tribute to his military service. They fired a volley of shots. A lone bugler played "Taps." An American flag was draped over his coffin. It was very moving. The priest said a prayer at the graveside and then talked a bit about what kind of man he was: He was a devoted family man and a hard worker. He drove a semitruck for Consolidated Freightways. He was named Truck Driver of the Year for 1973 by Teamsters Local 638, his union. He was very proud of that. All the years he drove a truck, he never had an accident. He was proud of that too. In fact, the only thing that ever happened to his truck was a dent on a trailer door from a hit-and-run—so it wasn't even his fault. His employers at Consolidated Freight gave him a gold watch when he retired. He treasured that watch and passed it on to my father.

After we buried my grandfather, my grandmother didn't want to live in their house in Wisconsin on Staples Lake, so she sold the place and moved back to Saint Paul. She eventually moved into one of my dad's apartment buildings on Thomas Avenue, but for a time after selling their place in Wisconsin, she lived with my parents. We kept a close eye on her. She was so sweet. And heartbroken.

During the whole ordeal of my grandfather's death, I was struck by how strong Dad was—handling details, taking care of business, just continuing to do what needed to be done, whatever was right in front of him. *If he can get through this, so can I.*

20

Third Arrest

About a week after my grandfather's funeral Dad returned to Las Vegas to drive my grandparents' car back to Saint Paul. My mother decided to go with him. I'm sure she needed a break.

My grandmother was staying at our house at the time, and she told my parents she'd watch over things. My younger sister, Jolynn, was thirteen years old at the time and my brother Jamie was just six, still a baby. My parents called to say they made it to Las Vegas just fine. They were staying with my dad's cousin. They told us to call if there were any developments with my case.

About two days into their trip, the phone rang at my parents' house. My grandmother answered. It was the lawyer. He said one of the victims who'd been present at the lineup returned to the police station. No one knows what transpired from the time of the police lineup to the day she returned, but she was now ready to state "with 99 percent certainty" that number three in the lineup was the man who had assaulted her. I was number three in that lineup. The police had issued a new warrant for my arrest.

My grandmother called my parents right away to tell them about the call. Dad's instructions were clear. "Tell Jay to hide."

"You want me to have him hide out from the police?" his mother asked.

"Yes. Until we get back there. They can wait. We'll go turn ourselves in then."

When I came home that evening my grandmother explained it to me. I couldn't believe what I was hearing. She was a nervous wreck. "Get out of the house. Now. They're on the way here to pick you up. Go!"

I went downstairs and threw some clothes in a bag. I contacted my cousin and told him I needed a place to stay for a few days. "Get over here," he told me.

Jody came over and announced, "I'm going with you."

"Be careful!" my grandma urged us both.

Jody and I left. We were officially on the lam.

In the essay she wrote about her perspective on this time of our lives, Mom explains my parents' reasoning for wanting me hide from the police:

> The day after we arrived in Las Vegas we received a phone call from Irene, Jerry's mother, that they wanted to arrest my son again. The authorities, we learned, were unhappy that we had bailed him out. They

wanted him under lock and key. Apparently,
another victim had identified him from
the lineup.

We could not let him just sit in jail again
without us there, without some support and
knowledge that we believed in him. We needed
to be there to assure him that everything
would be all right.

We also had no money to bail him out again.
We were in debt over twenty thousand
dollars—which was a great deal of money at
the time—what with the first bail we paid
and the attorney's twenty-five-hundred-dollar
retainer fee.

Jay would appear at the police station, but this
time we were going to bring him in. No more
police in front of our house with my son taken
away in handcuffs.

So, yes, I instructed my mother-in-law to have
my son go hide from the police.

Jody and I drove around for a while. We started dis-
cussing the situation and what our options were. We could
run away together. We could elope, get married, and go
hide out. Jody said if that's what I wanted, she'd do it. She
might have been calling my bluff. All I knew was I wanted
to be with this girl. I wanted to wake up from this nightmare. Going to prison for a long time for a crime I didn't

commit wasn't an option. For a while I had myself convinced I should just keep driving. I think it helped to just let my mind drift a little bit.

Eventually we showed up at my cousin's.

When we got there, he said, "Sit down, relax. There's beer in the fridge. I know what's going on, and it's bullshit. Try to take your mind off it."

I needed to hear those words right then.

That night some friends of my cousin's came over and a party sort of broke out. People were having fun, getting loose, without a care in the world. I remembered when my life had felt like that, carefree. Now it was just dark and heavy all the time. I couldn't go longer than a few moments without thinking about the accusations. It was torturous. I was trying to be strong, but I couldn't help but wonder, *Why me? What did I do to deserve this?*

All of a sudden I started getting emotional. I went into the living room, away from the party. Jody followed me. It all just washed over me, the dark reality of my life on the lam, my life as an adult criminal, how different it all looked now compared to the shiny future Jody and I had imagined for ourselves just a short time ago. I didn't see how it was ever going to get back to the way it was.

I had an emotional breakdown sitting on that couch with Jody. That's the only way I know how to describe it. I put my head down and started crying uncontrollably. I couldn't stop. I kept thinking about what I was being accused of—serial rape, an offense so horrific I could be going away for a long time to a terrible place, away from

Jody. All I could imagine was a lifetime of people thinking I was guilty. It was unbearable.

I felt sorry for myself and ashamed. I felt embarrassed for my family and for Jody. I felt awful for the financial burden this was placing on my parents. They weren't wealthy people. I felt bad for all those women who had been assaulted and raped.

My life would never be the same. I knew that now. The fear and shame and anger I'd been carrying around—it all came out. Those four days I spent in jail were the worst four days of my life. They treated me like a dog. I couldn't stand the thought of going back.

Jody let me cry. She wrapped her arms around me and said, "It's going to be all right, Jay. I'm with you no matter what happens." Those words meant everything to me. Then and now. She was my rock. I don't know what I would have done without her.

It took a while, but eventually I began to relax. Alcohol helped. After ten more minutes or so we went back into the party. I spent the rest of the night trying to drink away my misery.

On Monday my parents returned home, and my Dad called. "Pack it up," he said. "Time to go turn ourselves in." So off to jail we went again. My third time: once in juvenile detention for two days, once in the adult jail for four days, and now back for who knows how long. My parents were told this time I'd be in jail until the results of the semen, urine, and saliva test came back. They didn't say exactly how long that would be, but we learned that normally it only takes a few days to a week. In my case, it took twenty-eight days.

When my father paid ten thousand dollars for my last bail from the adult jail, he was told he'd get the ten thousand back from juvenile bail. That was money he planned to bail me out with again. He found out differently. He was told, "That money can't be released while the case is still pending." The lawyer tried everything in his power to try to get that money back, but the judge wouldn't budge.

"The judge is pretty sure Jay is the guy," he told my father.

With no money left to bail me out, I'd have to wait in jail until the forensic results came back.

Dad had some parting words for me when he dropped me off at jail. "Keep your head down, keep your mouth shut, and try not to be noticed."

This is not how it played out.

I was booked again, given a prison uniform, then led back down the long hallway to my new jail cell. I assumed my usual position on the top bunk. It's where I liked to be.

I looked out my window. *Hey, at least I have a view.*

21

The Big Marine

There are five degrees of criminal sexual assault according to current Minnesota laws, just as there were in 1982. The charge against Jay was criminal sexual conduct in the first degree, governed by Statute 609.343. The law reads that a person guilty of criminal sexual conduct in the first degree engages in "forcible sexual penetration (vaginal, oral, or anal sex or any intrusion of the victim's genital or anal openings by any part of the defendant or an object) of anyone, or sexual contact with a person under 13 (intentional touching of victim's bare genitals or anus by defendant or another's genitals or anus with sexual or aggressive intent) in the following circumstances:

- The victim is under 13 years old and the defendant is more than 3 years older than the victim

- The victim is 13 to 16 years old and the defendant is 4 years older and in a position of authority over

the victim (such as a parent, foster parent, psycho-
therapist, etc.)

- The circumstances placed the victim in reason-
able fear of imminent physical harm to himself or
herself or another

- The defendant was armed with a dangerous
weapon or threatened the victim with the weapon

- The defendant causes injury to the victim and
either uses force or coercion for sexual penetration or knows the victim is mentally or physically
impaired

- The defendant is helped by another person to
make the victim submit or the accomplice is
armed with a weapon

- The defendant has a significant relationship
(defendant is victim's parent, stepparent, guard-
ian, relative by blood, marriage, or adoption, or
an adult who lives in the same house and isn't the
victim's spouse) with the victim and the victim is
under 16 at time of sexual penetration

- The defendant engages in sexual intercourse with
another person by forcible compulsion where the
perpetrator:

    (a) Uses or threatens to use a deadly weapon or
    what appears to be a deadly weapon; or

    (b) Kidnaps the victim; or

    (c) Inflicts serious physical injury, including but

not limited to physical injury which renders the victim unconscious; or

(d) Feloniously enters into the building or vehicle where the victim is situated.

(e) Rape in the first degree is a class A felony."

Typically, a first-degree sexual assault conviction comes with a prison sentence of thirty years and a fine of forty thousand dollars. The mandatory minimum sentence is at least twelve years. Also, offenders are subject to conditional release, which means that for ten years after release from prison, the offender has to submit to sex offender treatment, monitoring, and so on. If the defendant had a prior sex offense conviction, he or she will be on conditional release for the remainder of his or her life.

These were the stakes weighing on Jay's mind as he settled in to prison for the third time.

Nothing was different about jail this time except that it was worse, not knowing how long I'd be there.

Each morning you had to help clean the dorm you were in. Each dorm held forty people. It gave me something to do. I also read the newspaper to pass the time. I tried to read books, but I couldn't concentrate. I walked a lot—just around the dorm. I was in another dimension. I remember thinking, *I just want to kill myself.* Every time I had that thought, I'd go walking and think about Jody.

Thinking about her is what kept me going every day.

As the days wore on I noticed people coming in and going out, getting released. Never me. Barely eighteen, I was the youngest guy in there. I was about one hundred and forty pounds with a slender build. I wasn't big at all. A couple of other guys around my age were there too—Rick and Jeff. They weren't very big either. We kind of hit it off. After being there a while you learn to find a few friends you think you can trust. I was already starting to think like an experienced convict. Jail is a scary place.

I knew Rick's uncle on the outside. He was a friend of my dad's. They drank together at the Trend Bar. The three of us would play cards to pass the time. We ate our meals together, and we made a kind of pact: if push ever comes to shove, we'll be there for each other, right? Rick and Jeff both said, "Hell yeah." I'd already seen a lot of shit in prison. Knowing I had a little backup was some comfort.

I told Rick and Jeff my story. They couldn't believe I was being accused of first-degree serial rape. I showed them a picture of Jody. They said she was "real pretty." I said we'd been going together for over a year, and we saw each other every day.

"And they think you raped sixteen women while you were doing that?" one of them asked.

They have no idea what it's doing to me, I remember thinking. *It's tearing me apart, mentally and physically. Maybe they do know.*

I understand how prisoners can quickly become full of rage.

During the first week I was there I received a visit from a neighborhood priest, Father Joe from St. Mark's Parish. At first I wasn't sure who arranged a visit from the local Catholic priest. Then he produced two letters from Jody that had her perfume on them, and I knew. I didn't think it was possible to miss someone as much as I missed Jody and my family, to be that lonely. This wasn't living. Father Joe told me I had to have faith. He encouraged me to pray. I went back to my cell. I stared out the window at the snow glistening in the moonlight for what seemed like hours. Then I got on my knees and I prayed. "Please, God, let this get straightened out. I feel like I'm losing my grip here a little. And look out for Jody and my family while I'm in here." Praying helped a little. I was grateful for Father Joe's visits.

One day a new prisoner showed up, a big marine. He seemed like a nice guy at first, telling stories and laughing. He said he'd gone AWOL and beat the shit out of somebody in a fight. That's what got him arrested on an assault charge. He definitely liked to be the center of attention.

After a few days he started to cop an attitude. His court date kept getting pushed back and he was getting mad. Then I think he decided he needed to establish himself as the alpha on the cellblock. So of course his eventual target was the youngest, smallest prisoner on the ward: me. He started calling me names. He called Rick and Jeff names too, but he definitely seemed to be concentrating on me. It began to get a little worse as time went by, so we reminded each other of our pact to keep an eye on each other.

"If anyone gives us shit, they'd be giving all three of us shit, right?" I asked them.

Rick and Jeff each replied, "That's right!"

One day the big marine took all my cigarettes and my candy. He just stole them from my cell. He stole things from Rick and Jeff too. I was mad as hell, so I told the guard. This is not something you're supposed to do in prison, snitch on each other.

The marine found out and the next day he called me a snitch and said he was going to "kick my fucking ass." I told him to fuck off. I have a hard time holding my tongue in situations like that. Plus I had a posse—I thought. I remembered my dad's advice to keep my head down and not get noticed. *I'm doing the best I can, Dad.*

The next day arrived and the big marine tried to take my milk from me at lunch. He just walked over to my table, put his hand on it, and started to take it. I yanked it back. "Oh hell no," I told him.

He pointed at me. "I'm gonna get you, snitch."

"Whatever." I tried to not show fear, but I was afraid.

I was constantly on the lookout. I had a pretty good idea what was coming. I asked Rick and Jeff, "If he tries anything, are you guys ready to go?"

"Hell yes!" one said.

"Let's get him," the other piped up.

Later that day I was standing in the commons area, where there was a TV. I looked up to the top of a spiral staircase, one story above, and there was the big marine, standing there, frozen, staring at me. He started down the steps. *Here we go. This is happening.*

Almost like they could smell it, other prisoners suddenly formed a circle around me and I could hear what they were saying.

"Kick his ass."

"Fuck him up."

"He's a snitch."

I looked up at the guard tower behind me. No guard. I suddenly realized I held Jody's picture in my hand. I carried it with me everywhere. I had no recollection of having pulled it out of my pocket—it was just there.

The marine walked straight toward me. As soon as he got near enough, without thinking about it, I hit him. I just made a fist, cocked my arm, and boom—as hard as I could, right between his eyes. I nailed him pretty good and his nose started to bleed. Then I put my head down and went at him, just swinging like a wild man, hitting him over and over, bam, bam, bam. He eventually knocked me backward. He was really strong.

I looked for my backup, Rick and Jeff. They were watching the fight with the rest of the gang.

One yelled, "Get him, Jay!"

The other added, "You got this!"

Clearly they wanted no part of the big marine. Then the marine had his arms around my head and was trying to knee me in the face. After three attempts, I grabbed for anything I could get my hands on and got his pinkie. I yanked on it as hard as I could. I heard it snap.

"Motherfucker! Shit! You broke my fucking finger. You bastard!"

Then guards were there, pulling us apart. The fight was over. I could feel my heart pounding a hundred miles a minute. Before I was taken away, I looked down and there it was, Jody's picture, lying on the ground. I picked it up and put it in my pocket.

Back at my cell door, Rick and Jeff came running over. "You really got that guy!" Rick said.

"Yes, I did. All by myself."

"You put it to him," Jeff said. "You really fucked him up."

I looked over their shoulders and saw some of the other guys on our pod, friends of the big marine. They were staring at me like a marked man, but a couple of them came up to me.

"You're bad, dude."

"You whupped his ass, showed him who's boss."

"Whatever," I replied.

I found out the big marine went to the hospital to get his broken finger fixed. The next time I saw him he had a big bandage on. "I'm gonna get you."

"Fuck you."

That fight earned me twenty-four hours in solitary—which wasn't much different from my cell—I just didn't have a view of the trains and the barges and the moonlight. I really missed that view.

After twenty-four hours in solitary I was moved to another cell on a different dorm. This one smelled like urine, but I found an unopened package of Camel cigarettes in my new cell. So at least I had that. I asked a guy in the new dorm for some matches and he gave me some. The cigarettes I found were unfiltered. Boy, you smoke one of those and you can catch a buzz if you're not used to them.

As I lit up, the guy who gave me the matches came over to my cell. "Hey, man, those guys in the other dorm are putting up signs saying you're a rapist. They're saying they're gonna kick your ass." I told the guy I was no rapist, and he seemed to believe me. But I was now a marked man in prison. Like things weren't bad enough.

I didn't get into any more fights. Nobody challenged me after that because word got out I'm not afraid to fight. If you fight, you get locked up for twenty-four hours. Nobody wanted that. But the rest of my time in jail was a living hell. I was constantly looking over my shoulder, wondering when I'd have to defend myself again. To be honest with you—that's something I still do today, look over my shoulder to make sure someone isn't about to jump me.

No one bothered me anymore. I guess I'd proven myself against the big marine.

The days passed at a snail's pace. I found myself trapped in a cycle of thinking that always led to a bad ending—me being labeled the Hillside Rapist and punished for someone else's crimes until the day I died. I was losing hope that my name would be cleared. Surely I would've been sprung by now if it was going to happen. I found myself wondering what kind of person I'd have to become to endure years of living like this, locked up. It was torture.

I wrote letters to Jody every day telling her how much I loved her. I never felt more lonely and helpless in my whole life. Knowing she was out there waiting for me was like a lifeline.

Then, on my twenty-eighth day in prison, it happened.

An announcement came over the prison loudspeaker: "Jay Perry Chapman to Control. Jay Perry Chapman to Control. Bring personal belongings." I thought I imagined it at first.

I was about the learn the results of the test they'd performed with my bodily fluids and the bodily fluids found on the victims of the Hillside Rapist, specifically those found on the older woman I'd faced in court, the older woman who'd named me with 99 percent certainty as her assailant.

All of a sudden a guard was at my cell to escort me. They didn't have to ask me twice. I left my cell for the last time and followed my escort to Control. On the way I walked down through my old cellblock and past the big marine. "I'm gonna get you on the outside, snitch."

"Fuck you," I told him.

It was April 2, 1982. I think I held my breath as we entered the glass-enclosed office they called Control. Dad was there. So was my lawyer.

"You can go," the guard told me. Then, with a fucked-up grin on his face, he said, "Good luck."

That's it. Five words. No explanation, no apology, no

follow-up, just "good luck."

None of us needed any further encouragement. We left.

My lawyer had a copy of the letter from the crime lab containing the results of the forensics examination, my ticket to freedom. The results had come out in my favor, though it had taken one month. He handed it to us in the parking lot: "For your records." I dropped it in the nearest trash can.

Dad and I hopped in his car and drove away. We didn't go home. My dad drove us to the Trend Bar. Taking me to his favorite watering hole was a rite of passage he'd always envisioned to commemorate his son's entry into manhood. He imagined it would happen when I was of legal drinking age, not after a one-month jail stint as an accused serial rapist. But there we were, drinking together for the first time. After we had a few rounds, my dad asked me what I wanted to do. "See Jody."

Dad would end his trips to the Trend, and all bars, soon after this eventful day. He realized his life depended on it. But I took his place at the bar for many years to come. The bar is where I took my feelings, frustrations, successes, and failures. I didn't dwell on them. I didn't talk about them. I drank them away. That stopped working for me eventually, just like it stopped working for my dad.

My dad drove us home, and I jumped in my car. I raced over to Jody's. I parked, walked up to her front door, and rang the bell—like I'd done many times before. It felt really different this time.

Her mother answered. I'd been worried about seeing her parents again. Jody's mom smiled. "Hi, Jay. Come on in. I'll go get Jody." She looked happy to see me. That meant the world to me.

Then Jody was there, coming down the steps, walking toward me at the front door, throwing her arms around me.

I'll never forget that day for as long as I live. She was so beautiful. She smelled so good. I gave her the biggest hug I've ever given anyone. I knew with certainty that I was very much in love with this girl and I always would be.

22

Evidence

The past few decades have seen great advances in a power-ful criminal justice tool: deoxyribonucleic acid, or DNA, the molecule that contains the genetic code of organisms. Your DNA is uniquely your own; it's nearly impossible for someone else to have your exact same DNA. The chances of one individual's DNA profile matching another person's are about one in a billion. It's mathematically possible for same-sex siblings to have the exact same DNA. Those chances are one in seventy million.

DNA analysis has been revolutionary as a crime-fighting tool, a game changer. It can be used to identify criminals with incredible accuracy when biological evidence exists. By the same token, it can be used to clear suspects and exonerate those mistakenly accused or convicted of crimes.

DNA is used to solve crimes in one of two ways. After

a suspect is identified, a sample of that person's DNA is compared to evidence from the crime scene. In cases where a suspect has not yet been identified, biological evidence from the crime scene can be analyzed and compared to offender profiles in the massive DNA databases that have been established. This has helped identify many perpetrators who thought they'd escaped scot-free.

All fifty states and the federal government have laws requiring that DNA samples be collected from all offenders in certain categories, and rape is at the top of that list. This practice has helped apprehend many rapists.

But in 1981 and early 1982, no such system was in place. The best practices of the day lay in matching bodily fluid types of the accuser and the accused, if samples were available.

This is how the Saint Paul police set out to prove that their prime suspect—their *only* suspect, Jay Chapman—was the Hillside Rapist.

According to the case file from the Ramsey County Criminal Lab, the following evidence was delivered to the Saint Paul police department in late February 1982:

Item 1: One test tube of blood from the victim.

Item 2: One test tube of blood from Jay Chapman.

Item 3: One white envelope said to contain saliva sample from victim.

Item 4: One white envelope said to contain rectal swab from victim.

Item 5: One brown paper bag said to contain clothing from victim.

Item 6: One brown paper bag said to contain clothing from Jay Chapman.

Item 7: One white envelope said to contain saliva from Jay Chapman.

The lab results were analyzed by a criminal laboratory specialist and sent to the chief of the Saint Paul police in a letter marked "confidential." Somehow, Jody Chapman procured a copy of the letter, which reads:

Examination of the blood (Item 1) and the saliva (Item 3) said to be from the victim revealed her to be **a secretor** of the International Blood Type O and PGH type 1+.

Examination of the blood (Item 2) and the saliva (Item 7) said to be from suspect Jay Perry Chapman revealed him to be **a non-secretor** of the International Blood Group Type A and PGM type 2-2+.

Examination of the rectal swab (Item 4) failed to reveal the presence of human seminal fluid.

Examination of the clothing (Item 5) said to be from the victim revealed the presence of human seminal fluid indicated to be from a secretor and PGM type 1+2+ and, therefore, **could not have come from Jay Perry Chapman.**

EVIDENCE

I hereby certify that the above report is true and accurate.

Signed,

Criminal Laboratory Analyst
April 2, 1982

Antigens are the molecules on the surface of every blood cell in your body. They are what determine your blood type. Nine out of ten people secrete their blood antigens into their bodily fluids. One out of ten does not.

While forensic evidence was often murky in pre-DNA investigations, this particular test comparing the bodily fluids of accused and accuser is as clear-cut as forensics examinations can be.

The victim whose biological evidence was tested against Jay's bodily fluids shared this description of her attacker: "white male, seventeen to eighteen years old, blondish, light brown, wavy hair, five foot six, one hundred forty to one hundred fifty pounds, full lips, 'baby face,' clean-shaven, reddish-maroon waist-length jacket, light blue jeans, and boots."

Her recollection of her attacker's physical characteristics is nearly identical to every other description of the Hillside Rapist, reinforcing the theory that a serial rapist—rather than multiple perpetrators—was responsible for the Cathedral Hill rapes of 1981 and 1982.

The physical description perfectly matches Jay Chapman at the time in all aspects but one: his blood antigens.

Jay doesn't secrete his blood antigens into his bodily

fluids. He's a non-secretor. He is one out of ten.

The Hillside Rapist does secrete blood antigens into his bodily fluids.

Therefore, Jay Chapman could not have been the rapist.

Tests like the one that ultimately cleared him generally yield results in one to four days. It's hard to know why Jay was kept in jail for a month.

Surely the Saint Paul police were bitterly disappointed when they learned they had the wrong guy locked up. The Hillside Rapist was still out there somewhere.

Letter from Jail

Day 26

Dear Jody,

It's a little after eight. I got up and ate breakfast for a change. I did some push-ups and some sit-ups. I am looking at your picture right now. I just can't get over how beautiful you look and how much you mean to me. I'm in love with you, Jody. You've taught me what the words mean. Thank you for staying with me through this. I can't wait to hold you in my arms again. I've been thinking about something. I can't forgive myself for that one night over at my house, that night I hit you. That was awful. I

promise you, Jody, I will *never* do anything like that again.
Ever.

I'm going to get this letter off and start writing you a
new one.

Love, Jay

23

Free

On April 2, 1982, after more than two months of living with the label serial rapist attached to his name, Jay Chapman was free—but only in a literal sense. "Good luck," were the only parting words he received from a criminal justice system that had turned his life inside out and upside down. The entire ordeal, from the Saint Paul police department's first visit to Jay's parents' home to Jay's release in the spring of 1982 lasted sixty-eight days. Thirty-three of those were in lockup.

Given that life-changing experience, returning to his old way of life wasn't going to be easy.

For a short period of time I thought I could pick up where I left off, go back to school, get on with my life.

Things had been going really well before all this happened. But word had spread like wildfire that I was the guy accused of those rape crimes. I heard people talking about me. I felt very trapped walking around school—almost like I was still in prison.

I talked to the one person at school I felt I could open up to, my teacher Johnny Bland. "I tell you what, Jay, I'm going to give you work you can do at home. I'll handle it on this end."

He didn't want me getting picked on at school. That could result in a fight and more trouble I really didn't need. Jody kept attending school while I stayed home and did the work Mr. Bland gave me. This was long before home schooling or remote learning was in practice. I thank God for Mr. Bland. He was there for me when I needed someone in my corner. I'll never forget his kindness. Because of him, I graduated from high school.

My close friends believed in me. They said they knew I was innocent, and they had my back. But a lot of other kids had their doubts. It's easier to latch onto a sensational story and run with it rather than take the time to learn all the facts. I went to keg parties after graduation at a lot of the old places like Hidden Falls, the Valley in Highland Park, and down by the Mississippi River. I heard whispers about me.

"That's the guy who was in jail for raping all those women."

"That's the guy they called the Hillside Rapist."

I noticed people standing apart from me and staring. Whispering. It was uncomfortable, but I kept showing up, hoping it would fade and things would return to normal. That's all I wanted, just to go back to how things were before. After about a year, I decided the hell with it. I stopped going to those parties. I stopped going a lot of places.

Jody and I did go to prom that year. I wasn't sure I wanted to attend, but it meant a lot to Jody, the girl who had stood by me in my darkest hours. I waited in her parents' living room for Jody to make her entrance in her new dress. Damn, she still took my breath away. *How blessed I am to have this girl in my life. A lot has gone wrong, but she is something that's very right.*

Prom was downtown again, near the Hill District, a part of town I now avoided. We danced and drank and stayed out all night and wound up having a wonderful time. But this was kind of how it was going to be for the rest of our lives together. Jody always wanted to go out, be part of the mainstream; I always wanted to lie back, hide a little, not be so exposed. As long as I had her by my side, I was OK. But I never felt comfortable again out in public. I still don't.

24

Peas in a Pod

"That's what everyone called us," said Jay. "Two peas in a pod. We were inseparable."

Jay and Jody graduated from Saint Paul Central High School and moved into an apartment together the following summer. The tiny apartment was above a bar called the House of Morgan in an area of the city known as Frogtown. Jay went to work for his dad at Chapman Construction Company. In the winter months, when construction work slowed, Jay picked up warehouse work. Jody went to school at St. Paul Technical Vocational Institute (TVI, now Saint Paul College) and studied bookkeeping. When she wasn't at school she was remodeling rooms at the Thunderbird Motel in Bloomington, a Twin Cities suburb. According to Jay, they were both hell-bent on making a go of it on their own.

Less than a year later they moved into a bigger Frogtown apartment in a house owned by Jay's parents. Jay began to work almost exclusively for his dad. It was work he loved, and he was getting very skilled at. It also paid well. Jody received her associate's degree from TVI and found accounting work at various companies over the next few years, including American Security (part of Marsden Services), Land O'Lakes, and the Vietnam Veterans of America.

When Jay turned twenty-one, he started his own siding business, Chapman & Company. This might have been a little too close to the name of his father's business, Chapman Construction Company, so Jay soon renamed his enterprise Final Touch Exteriors. His company still operates under that name today. Jay has a motto for the company: Beautify America.

A year later, he and Jody bought their first piece of property, a triplex on North Milton Street in Frogtown. They lived on the first floor for the next six years, renting out the rest of the house.

Jay's company quickly earned a reputation for doing quality work. He became known as a true professional with a great work ethic. Privately, a day didn't pass without Jay thinking about his ordeal as the alleged Hillside Rapist.

"I always felt I had something to prove," he said. "I never got over the idea that people were still talking about me, wondering if I was the guy who did all those terrible things."

Jody made it clear she wanted to be married. Jay made it clear he was committed to the relationship and always would be. Although his teenage self had written a letter from prison vowing that he wanted to marry her one day, he'd come to feel they didn't need a piece of paper to seal the deal. He adjusted his view on that again in 1988 when Jody announced she was pregnant. "It's time to make it official," she told Jay. He agreed.

On January 31, 1990, exactly ten years to the day after Jody walked into a high school party and knocked Jay off his feet, they were married in a downtown Saint Paul courtroom. In a stroke of irony, the ceremony was officiated by Judge J. Thomas Mott, formerly a public defender who'd briefly served as Jay's lawyer after his second arrest.

They named their baby girl Julia Rose. Two years later their second child arrived, a boy they named Jesse James. They bought a bigger house in Roseville on County Road B. This is the house they lived in for the rest of their married life. Jody settled in at home to raise her babies—what she'd always wanted to do—and Jay went to work.

Two years passed and Jay bought a home on Thomas Street in Saint Paul as an investment property. He paid for it with cash and put his professional stamp on the siding and the landscaping. He was following in his father's footsteps, buying property and fixing it up. When the house next to Jay and Jody's home came up for sale, Jay bought and rehabbed it as another investment property.

"The money was flowing," said Jay. "One month I brought home a paycheck of forty thousand dollars. We took trips and had nice cars. Life was good."

But Jody began to suspect, fairly early in the marriage, that when she and Jay struggled to communicate it might have something to do with the time in their lives when Jay was known as the Hillside Rapist. She thought counseling would help. But Jay just wanted to put it behind them.

"It's the most unpleasant thing that ever happened to me," Jay told her. "Why talk about it? To a stranger?"

Jody wanted to be free of the grip she felt the Hillside Rapist still had on them. Jay began working long hours and retiring to the garage after work so he wouldn't have to talk to anyone. That's when Jay hit on an idea.

"Maybe I should write a book," he told Jody. "Maybe that will set us free."

Jody thought it was a good idea.

She became tireless in her pursuit of the book, running down police records, making copies of diary entries, creating timelines, and writing query letters to agents and publishers.

Seventeen-year-old Jody had the proof in her diaries to clear Jay of the heinous crimes he'd been accused of and it wasn't allowed as evidence. She never got over that. Just as Jody was completing her research for the book, something else happened that she never got over. Jay calls it the beginning of the end of their marriage. He had an affair.

In the family tradition, Jay purchased a motor home as soon as he felt they could afford it. His dad had always owned one, and Jay had great memories of the trips they took while growing up. He wanted to create similar shared experiences for his family.

Jay's introduction to the drug methamphetamine happened around his and Jody's eleventh wedding anniversary in 2001. Jay was always the guy who had plenty of cash, which attracted a crowd of friends who liked to do drugs. His experimentation with meth coincided with selling his investment properties on Milton and Thomas Avenues. The sales put two hundred thousand dollars of cash in his pocket.

"After that," Jay reports, "I went a little nuts."

Meth took hold almost instantly, and Jay developed a daily habit. The family motor home proved a good place to party and use meth.

Then Jay met a woman through his new crowd of friends, and they began a drug-binging, sexual affair that lasted nine months.

"I just fell into it," Jay said. "I did things on drugs I never dreamed I'd ever do. That affair was one of them."

Accusations and denials ensued at home as Jay disappeared in the motor home for days and sometimes a week at a time. Then one day, Jody followed him as he drove away in the motor home. After it had been parked awhile, Jody burst in and found Jay and his mistress naked. She went after the other woman, and Jay had to physically restrain her from doing bodily harm.

That confrontation ended the affair. It also ended everything that had ever been good between Jody and Jay. She wanted to stay married until their kids graduated from high school. Jay wanted to stop using drugs and discovered he couldn't. So he worked and kept mostly to himself, going to the garage every night to drink in peace. Jody lost interest in their sex life and began stepping up her own drinking and occasional drug use. This is how they coexisted until 2006.

Then on a hot summer day Jay and Jody's seventeen-year-old daughter, Julia, called the police on her father. Jay was drunk and disorderly, high on meth, angry, shouting, and, according to the police report, "being threatening." He began breaking things in his house.

"I never hit anyone," Jay says. "I told Jody I would never do that again, and I meant it. I just broke stuff. A lot of stuff. I was out of my mind. These were my very crazy days."

When the police arrived, they told Jay to calm down. Apparently he didn't, because they tased him. Twice.

Jay was sentenced to seven days in the workhouse. That's when he began writing a first draft of this book. He also confirmed his love and gratitude for Jody, not wanting their marriage to be over. But it was too late for Jody.

Using her training in accounting, Jody had always managed the household finances. After Jay's stint in the workhouse, he decided to look into exactly how the money was being spent. He discovered Jody had been taking three hundred dollars a month off the top of each paycheck. When Jay asked where the money was going, Jody said she was putting it away for the kids. He was infuriated that she'd been doing that without consulting him. He went to the bank and took Jody's name off the account. Now Jody was furious.

"That was the final blow. We never recovered after that," Jay said.

This is the time, Jay says, that Jody seems to have given up. "She began drinking. Every day. I'd never known her to drink like that before. Vodka. Hiding bottles, everything."

On January 15, 2008, Jody moved out for good. The next day Jay quit meth and hasn't used it since. A month later Jody went to the doctor for what she thought was constipation and, shockingly, learned she was eight months pregnant.

If she'd had an inkling of her condition before that day, she'd kept it to herself.

Justin James, Jody and Jay's third child, was born in April 2008, eighteen years after their second baby. Justin lived with his mother for the first two years of his life. When it became apparent to Jay that Jody's drinking was getting out of hand, he petitioned the court for full custody. Jody said she'd contest it, but she failed to show up for the hearing. When a second hearing was scheduled, Jody showed up impaired by alcohol.

Jay was awarded full custody and has been a single parent to Justin ever since.

Jody soon remarried. "To an older man who drank," Jay says. Her new husband supplied the vodka Jody consumed to excess daily until the end of her life in 2016.

"The Hillside Rapist had a lot of victims," Jay says, considering how the repercussions of being wrongfully accused rippled through his life. "Jody was one of them."

25

Repercussions

RAINN (Rape, Abuse & Incest National Network) was founded in 1994 by Scott Berkowitz, a publisher and campaign manager. Berkowitz's friend was a social worker who counseled victims of sexual assault. One day she mentioned to him over lunch that she felt there was a big service gap in her industry. Experience told her that sexual assault and rape are much bigger problems than reporting reflects. She told him the nation needs a national hotline. Berkowitz, who knew nothing about the issue at the time, stepped in to help.

He set up a nationwide hotline for victims of sexual assault, bringing in singer Tori Amos, who has a personal connection to the issue, as the hotline's spokesperson. The rest is history.

The hotline exploded, and RAINN was born. Today it's the nation's largest antisexual violence organization.

RAINN operates the National Sexual Assault Hotline and is in partnership with more than a thousand local sexual assault service providers across the country.

RAINN also carries out numerous programs to prevent sexual violence, help survivors, and ensure that perpetrators are brought to justice.

The aftereffects of sexual assault and rape, according to RAINN, can be devastating, especially if left unaddressed. The most common aftereffect is depression, a disease that negatively affects how you feel, the way you think, and how you act. Depression can cause feelings of sadness and a loss of interest in almost everything. The emotional pain of a major depressive episode is such that many sufferers report an inability to function.

Another aftereffect is experiencing flashbacks, memories of the assault that can feel as if it's happening again. Flashbacks can hinder a victim's ability to be sexually intimate again.

Post-traumatic stress disorder (PTSD) is another aftereffect. PTSD often manifests as feelings of anxiety, stress, and fear that get so acute that victims have difficulty being around others for long periods of time.

Victims' journeys through shame and pain and back to self-love, safety, and security can be arduous, RAINN reports. They're journeys that are nearly impossible to travel alone. A strong support system is critical. Sexual assault survivors can't be reassured enough that what happened to them isn't their fault.

Rape and sexual assault survivors who don't know

where to turn have a number of available resources. The RAINN hotline is a good first call for help: **1-800.656. HOPE**.

RAINN has helped more than three million survivors, a big number but, sadly, just the tip of the iceberg. RAINN's dominant message is the advice to seek help if you're a victim. Don't attempt to navigate the resulting mental and emotional fallout by yourself.

Jody and Jay Chapman could have used this advice. They're a different kind of victim: the falsely accused.

False accusations of rape and sexual assault are rare. According to "False Allegations of Sexual Assault: An Analysis of Ten Years of Reported Cases," a 2010 study conducted by David Lisak, Lori Gardinier, Sarah C. Nicksa, and Ashley M. Cote, false allegations are a factor in between 2 and 10 percent of reported cases.

Mistaken accusations might be a more accurate label for a large portion of those that do occur. That's what happened in Jay's case: a mistaken accusation fueled by provoked confabulation.

Confabulation is simply the production of fictitious stories—making it up. It has puzzled clinicians for a long time. Recent studies have singled out spontaneous confabulation as a distinct disorder; it's more than simply lying. It's characterized by an inability to adapt thoughts and behavior to reality. The trauma of a sexual assault can actually alter your brain chemistry and the ability to differentiate between fiction and fact.

Far more common in criminal cases than spontaneous confabulation is *provoked* confabulation. This can happen when police lead the victim of a violent crime, such as a rape or sexual assault, to a prime suspect. The police evidence, mixed with their strong suspicions about a suspect's guilt, can sometimes cause the traumatized victim's brain to formulate memories that unconsciously conform to the police theory of events. The accuser will identify the suspect as the one who committed the crime based on traumatic memories, a psyche damaged by the attack, and the influence of exterior cues.

Police typically have reason to believe a prime suspect committed the crime. Jay Chapman, for example, was known to the police for various infractions; he'd had his picture taken and been written up; he lived near the scene of the crimes; he fit the description.

It's also possible that the immense pressure being applied by the community and the media was a factor in identifying a primary suspect before the police, desperate to make an arrest, were altogether ready to finger someone.

When this "evidence" is mixed with the traumatized confabulation of the victim, usually nothing but concrete evidence proving the accused's innocence can revert the charge. Once a traumatized victim has arrived at this conclusion, their belief can become unshakable. It's a form of survival.

Jay Chapman appears to have been the victim of a

mistaken accusation caused by provoked confabulation. All the ingredients were in play: a traumatized victim, an outraged community, an adamant police force, and a suspect who fit the description.

Compared to the extensive research about the aftereffects of sexual assault on victims, little has been written about the aftereffects of the experience of being falsely accused.

One example, though, is a study conducted by the Centre for Criminology at the University of Oxford. Researchers Ros Burnett, Carolyn Hoyle, and Naomi-Ellen Speechley looked at the phenomenon of false accusations against male sexual assault and rape suspects. They reported their findings in a 2017 issue of the *Howard Journal of Crime and Justice* in "The Context and Impact of Being Wrongly Accused of Abuse in Occupations of Trust." The study focuses on the aftermath—on what it's like to live as one who was accused and ultimately cleared. Most study participants had been accused of sexual assault of minors, but the study's theme is the miscarriage of justice and what it can do to a victim.

Jay Chapman wasn't part of this study—but he could have been, so similar are his symptoms to those of the men interviewed.

According to the study, the reputations of the accused men are damaged. After the relief of being cleared by concrete evidence, they often discover that the damage to their reputation remains and that returning to their previous normal is now impossible.

Participants in the Oxford study reported a variety of aftereffects, including high blood pressure, anxiety, insomnia, panic attacks, disturbed sleep and nightmares, and psychosomatic illness. One reported, "I am not the same person physically or mentally." Another shared, "I'm a much more serious, cynical person now and I'm not as trusting of others. I'm wary of people and their intentions." Another described his experience this way: "I cried more than I have ever cried in my life, mainly with anger but also with feeling so helpless." One study participant summarized, "I feel like I have become a failure."

The Oxford study mentions another aftereffect that directly relates to the suffering of Jody Chapman: "False allegations are also acutely felt by partners and family members, contributing to their own anxiety and depression."

The study goes on to explain how the stigma of a false allegation can lead to family breakdown if it goes unaddressed, permanently damaging relationships. It can also create financial conflict and burdens, and it can and lead to chronic abuse of alcohol and drugs.

One of the study participants elaborated on how the accusation impacted his relationship with a significant other. "Initially our relationship didn't change. I believe she knew I was innocent throughout, but over time I became more unstable and less confident. . . . We drifted apart, and she finally moved out."

Most of the participants reported having received no professional psychological support because they feared being judged or disbelieved by a counselor.

The study's concluding thoughts could be addressing Jody and Jay Chapman directly: "The lack of support, formal and informal, apology, or recognition of the pain caused to the accused was a constant theme. It resulted in deep mistrust of others, particularly those in authority (law enforcement) and a deep sense of alienation. . . . A false allegation is likely to affect *every aspect* of a person's life, psychological, material and physical. Most of the participants, it should be recalled, were able to refute the accusations made against them at a relatively early stage of the legal process. Despite this, their lives were, to put it simply, wrecked."

The study describes how being falsely accused can become definitive proof for many people: you were accused so you must be guilty.

Jay learned about that early after his release from jail. "Let's put it this way. I came to find out pretty quickly who my real friends were. And I didn't have many."

Jay Chapman's drive to finally share his story, after resisting any form of therapy for more than three decades, is a breakthrough. It's something his deceased soul mate, Jody, wanted to see happen in the worst way.

When Jody died, suddenly and way too soon, not only was Jay devastated, he was also deeply disappointed she hadn't lived to see the publication of their story. But he feels her presence, still. Jay believes she knows he rose up and said: *Enough. This story will be told.*

"I just wish it hadn't taken so long," Jay laments.

When Jay mentioned to family and friends that he was working on this book, their response was often to ask why he'd want to dredge up all that unpleasantness again.

Jay doesn't argue the point. He's been living with stigma, misunderstanding, doubt, and disbelief his entire adult life. He knows he can't change others' perceptions of who he is or—more accurately—who he isn't, but he can change his reaction to it.

The stigma of being labeled a rapist kept Jay from telling his story for a long time. He was afraid it would compound his pain. He intuitively knows that the fear of being stigmatized can prevent victims from seeking help, even from reporting the abuse, for the same reason: they don't want to compound their already unbearable pain. Jay hopes finally telling his story will, in some small way, help victims break free of the stigma, seek help, and ultimately be free.

"As bad as my suffering has been," Jay says, "I'm sure it's not as bad as the suffering of a victim of an actual sexual assault."

Resilience, a Chicago-based nonprofit organization, has been dedicated to the healing and empowerment of sexual assault survivors since 1974. Its website, ourresilience.org, has a Myths and Facts page that Jay thinks could help everyone—rape victims and all those who surround them, including friends, family, medical practitioners, social service workers, clergy, and law enforcement personnel.

The Resilience site dismantles some of the most common misconceptions about rape. For example, rape isn't the result of uncontrollable passion; it's an effort by a perpetrator to exert power and control over another.

Another myth about sexual assault is that if the victim didn't fight back, they must have wanted it. In fact, many victims of sexual assault experience a "freeze response" while they're being attacked so they can't move or speak.

And then there's the false notion that a person can't be raped by a spouse or a partner. According to Resilience, almost one out of ten women have experienced rape at the hands of an intimate partner.

Part of the larger cultural dialogue of sexual assault is a wariness about the potential for individuals to lie about being raped. However, the reality is that the rate of false reporting connected to sexual assault is the same as for other felony offenses: between 2 and 8 percent.

Perhaps the bleakest, head-in-the-sand myth is that rape does not happen that often. Actually, according to Resilience, each year in the United States, an average of 293,066 people ages 12 or older are the victims of rape or sexual assault. That's one sexual assault every one hundred seven seconds.

Source: Resilience, https://www.ourresilience.org/what-you-need-to-know/myths-and-facts/. Reprinted with permission.

Letter from Jail

Day 28

Dear Jody,

I got a feeling tomorrow is going to be the day. That blood test is coming back, and I just got a feeling it will be tomorrow. It has to be tomorrow. The test results will either set me free, or I'll be stuck here in this fucking jail. I hate this place. I'm not going to think about being stuck here. I'm going to read a few verses from *Good News for Modern Man*, the book Father Joe brought me cuz good news sounds all right to me.

I called school to see if I could talk to you. I talked to Kirkwood. What an asshole. He said no go.

I got your letter about forty minutes ago, Jody, and it took me twenty-five minutes to read it. I went really slowly. I kept reading stuff over and over. I didn't want it to end. I'll probably read it a hundred times until your next one gets here.

I'm sorry you're having so many problems with your family.

I dreamt about us last night. We were at my family's cabin. We were alone, and we were making love. It was a great dream.

I want you so bad. And when I do get you, it will be the best and the longest and the hardest and the deepest ever.

Guys here talk a lot of shit. They say girls don't wait for guys in jail. I just laugh at them. They don't know how much you love me and that I love you more than anything else in the whole world and always will.

For dinner we had turkey, dressing, salad, apple pie, and chocolate milk. I ate it all, and now I feel like I'm going to throw up.

That test has to come tomorrow. I need to see your face again.

I'm out of things to say.

That's it.

I love you.

And I mean it.

Jay

Note: This letter was written the day Jay Chapman was released from jail.

26

Today

Jay and his youngest son, Justin, live in Roseville, the only suburb in the Twin Cities that butts up against both Minneapolis and Saint Paul. Roseville is where they built the first Target store. The first Dairy Queen too. Its most famous former residents are all named Anderson: Richard Dean Anderson who starred in *MacGyver*, Loni Anderson who starred in *WKRP in Cincinnati*, New Jersey Devils winger Joey Anderson, and Los Angeles Kings defenseman Mikey Anderson.

Jay is proud of how far he's come professionally and personally. His siding business is thriving. He has a five-star review with the Better Business Bureau and glowing testimonials.

Justin comes to the work site with his dad fairly often, just like Jay did when he was a kid. Justin is twelve years old, in school, and "doing all right," according to Jay.

Justin struggles with concentration and memory as a result of mild fetal alcohol syndrome but otherwise is highly functioning. He's happy and healthy and Jay is devoted to him.

Jay likes to have family around.

"They are my number one priority," he says.

He remains close to his older children, Julia, who is busy raising her three children (Jordyn, Jayde, Jayla) and Jesse, who works for Jay and provides for his daughter, Kaylene.

The family spends a lot of time at Jay's home in Roseville. The trips in the motor home never stopped.

"We love camping," said Jay, "floating down rivers, being outdoors."

In the winter, trips in the motor home to warmer climes are not uncommon. Jay is a history buff, so when he's on the road he likes to visit museums. And he exercises every day as a way of helping him stay clean and sober. But he still smokes cigarettes. "I'm gonna quit," Jay says, "I got to. I hate smoking. It's time to get this monkey off my back. I have a lot to live for."

After a long, self-imposed solitude, Jay Chapman has been dating recently. Like many, he's trying to meet someone through an online dating service. Jay describes himself as a "one-woman family man." He prefers being in a committed relationship, and he's slowly but surely putting himself out there again.

Jay doesn't mention to new friends that time of his life, almost forty years ago, when he was called the Hillside

Rapist. He knows that, eventually, if anything develops into a serious relationship, he'll have to talk about it. He also knows the mere suggestion of having the label *rapist* attached to his name can end a potential relationship before it even begins. So he goes slowly.

"I try to be positive and truthful, always," Jay says. "I try to be kind to all people, treat them how I want to be treated. I try to learn from my mistakes."

The stigma of the label *rapist* will never be a thing of the past for Jay. Not fully. That is not fair but Jay has learned to live with unfair. It's the reason he is still alive. It's a big part of the reason Jody isn't alive. She devoted most of her adult life to clearing her family's name, to move out from under the shadow of a heinous accusation. It's a fight she lost.

Jay has finally learned to live with that as well. "She was definitely my soul mate," Jay says. "I am a lucky man to have met my soul mate."

Jay took a recent date to a local brewery. The establishment on this particular night had a band on stage and the dance floor was rocking. Jay and his date danced the night away.

The band's encore was a song titled "Tubthumping," by the 1990s British rock band Chumbawamba. Jay has always liked that song. He has a special connection to the song's chorus about getting knocked down and getting up again. "You're never gonna keep me down," the song insists.

Jay had a secret smile on his face as he danced and

sang along to these lyrics. He has been knocked down so many times in his life he has stopped counting.

But he's back on his feet again. He's even dancing a little bit now and then.

And while the specter of the Hillside Rapist is Jay's unwelcome lifelong companion, he can go long periods of time now without acknowledging his existence.

And he knows the Hillside Rapist for what he is: a deviant, a thief, and a coward, nothing like Jay Chapman.

27

Aftermath

No other sexual assaults or rapes occurred in the Hill District of Saint Paul in the immediate aftermath of Jay Chapman's highly publicized series of arrests and subsequent imprisonment. Many in the community refused to believe Jay wasn't the Hillside Rapist and were furious when he was released.

Just prior to publication of this book, the Saint Paul police department was contacted about the 1981–82 case known as the Hillside Rapes. Jay was never informed if an arrest was made after he was freed, and he's never asked. Jay wanted to put the entire episode behind him immediately, the sooner the better. So did Jody. So did the entire Chapman family.

A representative of the Sexual Assaults and the Cold Case division of the police department was very helpful. She stated she hadn't heard about this thirty-eight-year-old case, but she'd do some research and follow up.

Three days later, she called back and said, "According to our records, an arrest was made in the 1981/1982 case of the serial rapist you called about—the Hillside Rapist. That isn't what we call it here," she said, "but it's the case you are referring to."

"The man arrested (Jay Perry Chapman) was jailed but was subsequently released after forensic tests determined he wasn't the perpetrator. No other arrest was ever made in relation to that case. The criminal was never apprehended."

Acknowledgments

Jay Chapman would like to acknowledge the following for their unwavering support in the creation of this book:

Jody Chapman

Jerry and Judee Chapman

Julia Chapman

Jesse Chapman

Justin Chapman

Tim Reidell

About the Authors

Jay Chapman is the owner and founder of Final Touch Exterior Inc., a siding company in St. Paul, Minnesota, that has been in operation for thirty-six years. When Jay is not "beautifying America one home at a time" (his company's slogan), he is traveling America in his RV with his thirteen-year-old son, Justin. Jay lives in Roseville, Minnesota.

Patrick Coyle is a writer, actor, director, and adjunct professor of film at Minneapolis College and the Minneapolis College of Art and Design. He lives in St. Paul, Minnesota.